BIBLE
CRYPTOGRAMS

Over 400 Puzzles!

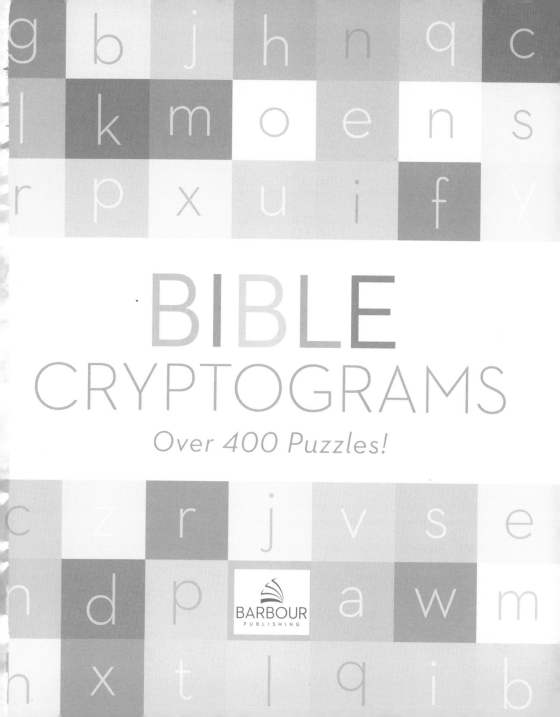

BARBOUR
PUBLISHING

Puzzles edited by Jennifer Hahn.

ISBN 978-1-64352-733-8

All scripture quotations are taken from the King James Version of the Bible.

Published by Barbour Publishing, Inc., 1810 Barbour Drive, Uhrichsville, Ohio 44683, www.barbourbooks.com

Our mission is to inspire the world with the life-changing message of the Bible.

 Member of the
Evangelical Christian
Publishers Association

Printed in China.

Welcome to
BIBLE CRYPTOGRAMS!

If you like cryptograms, you'll love this book. Here are 404 Bible-based puzzles to expand your knowledge of God's Word and test your puzzle-solving skills, as thousands of encoded letters—all in verses taken from the King James Version of the Bible—await you.

Each cryptogram is a verse in substitution code. For example, JEHOVAH might become MPXSTQX if M is substituted for J, P for E, X for H, and so on. One way to break the code is to look for repeated letters: E, T, A, O, N, R, and I are the most often used. Single letters are usually A or I, and OF, IT, and IS are common two-letter words. Try THE and AND for three-letter groups. The puzzle titles and the scripture references may give you additional direction, and—if you want even more help—we've provided a substitution clue with each puzzle. Remember that the code is different for each Bible cryptogram. Answers, of course, can be found in the back of the book.

We know you're eager to get started, so just one final word: Enjoy!

1

BORN AGAIN!

ZGB Q OH YGC OVJOHKR GZ CJK LGVFKS GZ WJBQVC: ZGB QC

QV CJK FGMKB GZ LGR NYCG VOSXOCQGY CG KXKBI GYK CJOC

AKSQKXKCJ; CG CJK TKM ZQBVC, OYR OSVG CG CJK LBKKP.

BGHOYV 1:16   *Clue: L = G*

KGF YA PHA KUGJE FU RXNA FMPJQW PBYPC FU RUE VUH

CUG, KHAFMHAJ KABUNAE UV FMA BUHE, KATPGWA RUE MPFM

VHUD FMA KARXJJXJR TMUWAJ CUG FU WPBNPFXUJ FMHUGRM

WPJTFXVXTPFXUJ UV FMA WZXHXF PJE KABXAV UV FMA FHGFM.

2 FMAWWPBUJXPJW 2:13   *Clue: C = Y*

THE KEY INGREDIENT

URM ATGZG GUVM ZRHN QVK, CN HQD FUD; HQD IUVHQ QUHQ

KUMT HQTT FQNOT. URM VKKTMVUHTOD QT JTETVLTM QVG

GVCQH, URM INOONFTM ATGZG VR HQT FUD.

KUJX 10:52   Clue: O = L

KUG CYVGVXW XL CYV GXHYCVUQLWVLL UK HUB GVPVRDVB

KGUS KRXCY CU KRXCY: RL XC XL JGXCCVW, CYV TQLC LYRDD

DXPV OF KRXCY.

GUSRWL 1:17   Clue: Y = H

A WING AND A PRAYER

CVZ RCVU GR BRQFDBX FR F LGZX CVE CK ESB RMFZB CK ESB

KCHUBZR: ESB RMFZB GR LZCNBM, FMX HB FZB BRQFDBX.

DRFUA 124:7   *Clue: V = U*

TDVOL ERA AJL GKEF, ER ERA KE AJU AJRDFJA; NES TDVOL ERA

AJL VKTJ KE AJU HLSTJNPHLV: MRV N HKVS RM AJL NKV OJNXX

TNVVU AJL ZRKTL, NES AJNA BJKTJ JNAJ BKEFO OJNXX ALXX AJL

PNAALV.

LTTXLOKNOALO 10:20   *Clue: F = G*

A VERY IMPORTANT PERSON

ZLC JRV URXEC FWVB, ZLC PRV YWITFRJ RXO TLJI KRZWZIR'P

CZTFRJVW, ZLC RV YVUZOV RVW PIL. ZLC PRV UZEEVC RXP LZOV

OIPVP: ZLC PRV PZXC, YVUZTPV X CWVB RXO ITJ IQ JRV BZJVW.

VDICTP 2:10   *Clue: O = M*

DZ GPSMY CNBKB, LYKO YK LPB ANCK MN ZKPWB, WKGTBKI MN

DK APRRKI MYK BNO NG HYPWPNY'B IPTQYMKW; AYNNBSOQ

WPMYKW MN BTGGKW PGGRSAMSNO LSMY MYK HKNHRK NG QNI,

MYPO MN KOXNZ MYK HRKPBTWKB NG BSO GNW P BKPBNO.

YKDWKLB 11:24–25   *Clue: A = C*

FDMWAI, PMD DCD WB PMD AWSI NZ XEWT PMDG PMKP BDKS

MNG, XEWT PMDG PMKP MWED NT MNZ GDSLC.

EZKAG 33:18   *Clue: W = O*

AXTZZTU AT CDT IEU OPU WOCDTY EW ENY XEYU GTZNZ KDYJZC,

QDJKD OKKEYUJPI CE DJZ OANPUOPC FTYKB DOCD ATIECCTP NZ

OIOJP NPCE O XJLTXB DEVT AB CDT YTZNYYTKCJEP EW GTZNZ

KDYJZC WYEF CDT UTOU.

1 VTCTY 1:3   *Clue: A = B*

MVF FKRM WKRH IPF WKR SVUOMRII VC NRWRT PMO EVKM, PMO

NRTJRGZRO WKPW WKRH FRTR BMURPTMRO PMO GQMVTPMW

LRM, WKRH LPTZRUURO; PMO WKRH WVVY YMVFUROQR VC

WKRL, WKPW WKRH KPO SRRM FGWK ERIBI.

PJWI 4:13   *Clue: U = L*

UHP EUQQSUFRB BVAAP, UHP BULP RHVA VSF NAWP: CFSANP,

NAWP, VSF SUNG AG XD TAAPB L TLOF VA VSF ZAAW; UHP

LG L SUOF VUIFH UHD VSLHT GWAX UHD XUH CD GUNBF

UQQRBUVLAH, L WFBVAWF SLX GARWGANP. UHP KFBRB BULP

RHVA SLX, VSLB PUD LB BUNOUVLAH QAXF VA VSLB SARBF.

NRIF 19:8—9   *Clue: O = V*

POWERFUL STUFF

OS IYBE KEVUJVAP BWAY APV FBIA: RBCKDVW APYB OV

UKKYLFCWX AY APS NYLF.

QIUEO 119:25   *Clue: W = N*

YPF LUW NPFA PY BPA CH GVCQZ, TEA RPNWFYVJ, TEA HUTFRWF

LUTE TEO LNPWABWA HNPFA, RCWFQCEB WMWE LP LUW

ACMCACEB THVEAWF PY HPVJ TEA HRCFCL, TEA PY LUW KPCELH

TEA DTFFPN, TEA CH T ACHQWFEWF PY LUW LUPVBULH TEA

CELWELH PY LUW UWTFL.

UWXFWNH 4:12   *Clue: Y = F*

GOOD KINGS

MCL WTVQ LYL TZXZGYMT WTAIVUTIVW MFF KVLMT, MCL

JAIVUTW WTMW JTYPT JMQ UIIL MCL AYUTW MCL WAVWT SZEIAZ

WTZ FIAL TYQ UIL.

2 PTAICYPFZQ 31:20   Clue: A = R

BCS WVTEBO PVVA BLBI BRR POG BKVQECBPEVCT VXP VM

BRR POG YVXCPJEGT POBP FGJPBECGS PV POG YOERSJGC VM

ETJBGR, BCS QBSG BRR POBP LGJG FJGTGCP EC ETJBGR PV

TGJZG, GZGC PV TGJZG POG RVJS POGEJ HVS.

2 YOJVCEYRGT 34:33   Clue: S = D

9
BAD KINGS

FWA GY RKR AGUA LGKIG LUP YBKT KQ AGY PKJGA SD AGY TSCR,

UP RKR ZUQUPPYG GKP DUAGYC: DSC UZSQ PUICKDKIYR WQAS

UTT AGY IUCBYR KZUJYP LGKIG ZUQUPPYG GKP DUAGYC GUR

ZURY, UQR PYCBYR AGYZ.

2 IGCSQKITYP 33:22   *Clue: Z = M*

CGQ CYCF DYN PZG ZU ZWKT QTQ NBTH TG DYN PTMYD ZU DYN

HZKQ CFZBN CHH DYCD RNKN FNUZKN YTW.

1 VTGMP 16:30   *Clue: F = B*

SPIRITUAL FRUIT

VLVJ YP VLVCI TPPG BCVV ZCSJTVBD KPCBD TPPG KCMSB; ZMB X

QPCCMAB BCVV ZCSJTVBD KPCBD VLSR KCMSB.

FXBBDVU 7:17   *Clue: T = G*

GAU WFY GHCWE SXNH TBHH TBFS RCW, XWN GHQFSH

RHBIXWUR UF EFN, LH OXIH LFAB TBACU AWUF OFJCWHRR, XWN

UOH HWN HIHBJXRUCWE JCTH.

BFSXWR 6:22   *Clue: G = B*

SIMON SAYS

NVC YJKGV FHRHO NVYZHOHC NVC YNJC, RAGD NOR RAH

SAOJYR, RAH YGV GQ RAH XJPJVM MGC.

KNRRAHZ 16:16   *Clue: V = N*

OVFVA EHBT ZPFI QBJ, UIAT, KQM NHPPIF B RIUUIK FQVV PIK? B

KBUU UHM TIKP JM UBRV RIA FQM EHWV.

GIQP 13:37   *Clue: K = W*

THE FLOOD

MUB FAB PMGB WUCA UAMD, CDY YUB AH MNN HNYPD GP

SAEY VYHALY EY; HAL CDY YMLCD GP HGNNYB OGCD RGANYUSY

CDLAWFD CDYE; MUB, VYDANB, G OGNN BYPCLAT CDYE OGCD

CDY YMLCD.

FYUYPGP 6:13   *Clue: H = F*

JBY BIJA YKY JWWIZYKBC VBNI JQQ NAJN NAD QIZY WIUUJBYDY

AKU.

CDBDRKR 7:5   *Clue: N = T*

JCA YLI STGA DJBA OCYT FTDID, DYGIYZL TOY YLBCI LJCA

YTXJGA LIJEIC, YLJY YLIGI FJH WI AJGQCIDD TEIG YLI SJCA TV

IMHRY, IEIC AJGQCIDD XLBZL FJH WI VISY.

IUTAOD 10:21   *Clue: F = M*

BRJ QH PBZK HA TBMM, BM HDKX SKOK LIOXQRU

B ZBR, HDBH, LKDAGJ, HDKX MTQKJ B LBRJ AV

ZKR; BRJ HDKX PBMH HDK ZBR QRHA HDK MKTIGPDOK

AV KGQMDB: BRJ SDKR HDK ZBR SBM GKH JASR, BRJ

HAIPDKJ HDK LARKM AV KGQMDB, DK OKNQNKJ,

BRJ MHAAJ IT AR DQM VKKH.

2 EQRUM 13:21   *Clue: L = B*

LCK TLCR PE USHT USLU MBHHW FC USH KOMU PE USH HLZUS

MSLBB LJLVH, MPTH UP HQHZBLMUFCA BFEH, LCK MPTH UP

MSLTH LCK HQHZBLMUFCA DPCUHTWU.

KLCFHB 12:2   *Clue: T = M*

JOV R BJM J ONM FNJCNO JOV J ONM NJYUF: KHY UFN KRYBU

FNJCNO JOV UFN KRYBU NJYUF MNYN DJBBNV JMJW; JOV

UFNYN MJB OH SHYN BNJ.

YNCNXJURHO 21:1   *Clue: M = W*

GREAT STUFF FROM THE PSALMS

SYH OWB CYHV ZKYIBOW OWB IUQ YS OWB HPTWOBYNJ: GNO

OWB IUQ YS OWB NKTYVCQ JWUCC ABHPJW.

AJUCE 1:6   *Clue: Q = Y*

CH CF W PLLG HOCAP HL PCZS HOWARF XAHL HOS YLQG, WAG

HL FCAP DQWCFSF XAHL HOK AWUS, L ULFH OCPO: HL FOSN

ILQHO HOK YLZCAPRCAGASFF CA HOS ULQACAP, WAG HOK

IWCHOIXYASFF SZSQK ACPOH.

DFWYU 92:1–2   *Clue: P = G*

SJBOB TE M OTRBO, SJB ESOBMDE QJBOBIP EJMZZ DMFB HZMV

SJB UTSG IP HIV, SJB JIZG WZMUB IP SJB SMKBOLMUZBE IP SJB

DIES JTHJ.

WEMZD 46:4

Clue: M = A

GATRPB KB NSB IWAY. GATRPB EWY RC SRP

PTCLNZTAK: GATRPB SRX RC NSB HRAXTXBCN WH SRP GWOBA.

GATRPB SRX HWA SRP XRESNK TLNP: GATRPB SRX TLLWAYRCE NW

SRP BULBIIBCN EABTNCBPP.

GPTIX 150:1–2

Clue: L = C

JOHN THE BAPTIST

IRT U ECP QKBR PRQ, CYRKL BOREJ BOCB CTJ DRTK RI FRYJK

BOJTJ UE KRB C LTJCBJT ATRAOJB BOCK VROK BOJ DCABUEB:

DQB OJ BOCB UE SJCEB UK BOJ XUKLMRY RI LRM UE LTJCBJT

BOCK OJ.

SQXJ 7:28   *Clue: L = G*

JFS HFIY VIO ADTVERV WDPO YOEVIOS ODVEYQ ASODL YFS

LSEYZEYQ MEYO; DYL UO RDU, IO IDVI D LOXEC. VIO RFY FJ

PDY ER WFPO ODVEYQ DYL LSEYZEYQ; DYL UO RDU, AOIFCL D

QCBVVFYFBR PDY, DYL D MEYOAEAAOS, D JSEOYL FJ TBACEWDYR

DYL REYYOSR!

CBZO 7:33–34   *Clue: A = B*

PRECIOUS METALS

CJ NMUHH TAP YUFJ QWPM YJ EAKN AG NWHXJO, TJWPMJO

NMUHH CJ YUFJ BTPA CAB EAKN AG EAHK.

JSAKBN 20:23

Clue: U = A

SBT CVJ CQJDPJ ISCJG QJMJ CQJDPJ EJSMDG: JPJMR GJPJMSD

ISCJ QSG YX YBJ EJSMD: SBT CVJ GCMJJC YX CVJ LHCR QSG

EFMJ IYDT, SG HC QJMJ CMSBGESMJBC IDSGG.

MJPJDSCHYB 21:21

Clue: I = G

XZJ NC MWW NHFMLW JKLFL BMH CDCL JD XL HD SZPK

UFMNHLY MH MXHMWDS EDF KNH XLMZJV: EFDS JKL HDWL DE

KNH EDDJ LGLC JD JKL PFDBC DE KNH KLMY JKLFL BMH CD

XWLSNHK NC KNS.

2 HMSZLW 14:25   *Clue: C = N*

DRU SL XNAFMSV FJ SDUDCCDS, VSDV HC, LCVSLN, SHC FRZWL'C

UDFMSVLN: GAN CSL SDU RLHVSLN GDVSLN RAN PAVSLN, DRU

VSL PDHU YDC GDHN DRU XLDFVHGFW; YSAP PANULZDH, YSLR

SLN GDVSLN DRU PAVSLN YLNL ULDU, VAAO GAN SHC AYR

UDFMSVLN.

LCVSLN 2:7   *Clue: G = F*

RXG SN URLG, SNRH XBD CF DBHGU: LY ASNHN IN R MHBMSNA

RCBXP FBW, L ASN JBHG DLJJ CRON CFUNJY OXBDX WXAB SLC

LX R TLULBX, RXG DLJJ UMNRO WXAB SLC LX R GHNRC.

XWCINHU 12:6

Clue: M = P

QWC CJY LDSLJYC, NJUAJ TJKEE LDYTWGY CS TLYKM K NSDR UI

GX IKGY, NJUAJ U JKOY ISC ASGGKIRYR JUG CS TLYKM, SD CJKC

TJKEE TLYKM UI CJY IKGY SH SCJYD VSRT, YOYI CJKC LDSLJYC

TJKEE RUY.

RYWCYDSISGX 18:20

Clue: G = M

PROPHETS IN SPECIFIC

SOV PLYD PZGV PLY MWOI, HSDWOI, NYLZGV OSPLSO PLY

AFZALYP. SOV JLYO LY JSH UZBY WO NYRZFY PLY MWOI, LY

NZJYV LWBHYGR NYRZFY PLY MWOI JWPL LWH RSUY PZ PLY

IFZXOV.

1 MWOIH 1:23   *Clue: I = G*

YCI FCWX YUFV QL OLVILLW VIC CNSWSCWG? ST VYL FCZP OL

XCP, TCFFCI YSA: OJV ST OUUF, VYLW TCFFCI YSA. UWP VYL

NLCNFL UWGILZLP YSA WCV U ICZP. VYLW GUSP LFSMUY JWVC

VYL NLCNFL, S, LHLW S CWFQ, ZLAUSW U NZCNYLV CT VYL

FCZP; OJV OUUF'G NZCNYLVG UZL TCJZ YJWPZLP UWP TSTVQ

ALW.

1 ESWXG 18:21–22   *Clue: O = B*

SJ DFGRK OXQR IXR FKMKNSXF RSBN EJDG OKXDF. XJO SRXSXF

DFK HLGHFKD DFK RGJ GV XUGM BXUK EJDG FSU, XJO RXSO

EJDG FSU, DFER RXSDF DFK CGLO, RKD DFSJK FGERK SJ GLOKL:

VGL DFGE RFXCD OSK, XJO JGD CSAK.

SRXSXF 38:1   *Clue: E = U*

AIAD SBA HCTHBAS MACAQWNB RNWP, NQAD: SBA YTCP PT RT:

SBA YTCP HACKTCQ SBU XTCPR XBWZB SBTV BNRS HCTHBARWAP,

ST ECWDL NLNWD SBA IARRAYR TK SBA YTCP'R BTVRA, NDP NYY

SBNS WR ZNCCWAP NXNU ZNHSWIA, KCTQ ENEUYTD WDST SBWR

HYNZA.

MACAQWNB 28:6   *Clue: E = B*

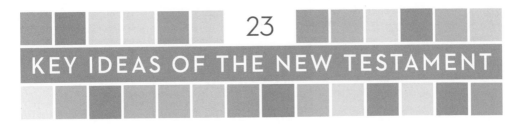

TNO IDRMR SMR GPFRMUPIPRU NA LPAIU, HQI IDR USZR UBPMPI.

STG IDRMR SMR GPAARMRTKRU NA SGZPTPUIMSIPNTU, HQI IDR

USZR VNMG. STG IDRMR SMR GPFRMUPIPRU NA NBRMSIPNTU, HQI

PI PU IDR USZR LNG ODPKD ONMERID SVV PT SVV.

1 KNMPTIDPSTU 12:4—6   *Clue: O = W*

OCE HQHWM VWNHPK PKOCEHKL EONXM FNCNPKHWNCA OCE

YBBHWNCA YBKHCKNFHP KLH POFH POSWNBNSHP, ULNSL SOC

CHQHW KOIH OUOM PNCP: DJK KLNP FOC, OBKHW LH LOE

YBBHWHE YCH POSWNBNSH BYW PNCP BYW HQHW, POK EYUC

YC KLH WNALK LOCE YB AYE.

LHDWHUP 10:11—12   *Clue: A = G*

CLEANLINESS IS NEXT TO GODLINESS

NS FNWEE KNSVSPRVS JAVG KNWK HWVOSGK, CNSKNSV CWVZ

RV CRRP, LG CRREESG RV LG ELGSG, RV WGQ KNLGH RP FBLG,

CNSVSLG KNS ZEWHAS LF: PRV LK LF W PVSKKLGH ESZVRFQ; LK

FNWEE JS JAVGK LG KNS PLVS.

ESYLKLXAF 13:52

Clue: E = L

KCE VNS DSJSL OC BNTI VNS JDKYRS OQ, NOQ HDTVNSQ QNKDD FS

LSCV, KCE NOQ NSKE FKLS, KCE NS QNKDD JRV K HTGSLOCY RJTC

NOQ RJJSL DOJ, KCE QNKDD HLU, RCHDSKC, RCHDSKC. KDD VNS EKUQ

BNSLSOC VNS JDKYRS QNKDD FS OC NOI NS QNKDD FS ESXODSE; NS

OQ RCHDSKC: NS QNKDD EBSDD KDTCS.

DSGOVOHRQ 13:45–46

Clue: R = U

VERSES WORTH MEMORIZING

YDI QWG UWNNJLGJIF FKA HWZJ IWPRBG DA, KL IFRI, PFKHJ PJ

PJBJ CJI AKLLJBA, UFBKAI GKJG XWB DA.

BWNRLA 5:8

Clue: U = C

WB MHK CBZBLXBC; YHC LE MHK VHZDBC: OHU QJFKEHBXBU F

VFM EHQBKJ, KJFK EJFPP JB FPEH UBFR. OHU JB KJFK EHQBKJ

KH JLE OPBEJ EJFPP HO KJB OPBEJ UBFR ZHUUIRKLHM; WIK JB

KJFK EHQBKJ KH KJB ERLULK EJFPP HO KJB ERLULK UBFR PLOB

BXBUPFEKLMY.

YFPFKLFME 6:7–8

Clue: R = P

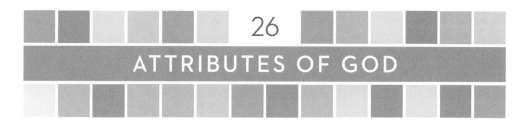
PUO TPHU HJG DWPR GHGMPIE, WLLUMHIE, WPSWAWCEG, HJG

UPEN OWAG RUK, CG JUPUTM IPK REUMN ZUM GSGM IPK GSGM.

ILGP.

1 HWLUHJN 1:17   *Clue: P = N*

JIPL GUOP JIP CWST WK JIP DWST XLJW YPSPOFUI, EUNFLB,

HPIWDT, F UO JIP DWST, JIP BWT WK UDD KDPEI: FE JIPSP ULN

JIFLB JWW IUST KWS OP?

YPSPOFUI 32:26–27   *Clue: O = M*

REAL SMARTS

BDY LYJX SL BDY USXF VA BDY IYWVHHVHW SL PVAFSG: J WSSF

CHFYXABJHFVHW DJNY JUU BDYR BDJB FS DVA QSGGJHFGYHBA:

DVA TXJVAY YHFCXYBD LSX YNYX.

TAJUG 111:10   *Clue: W = G*

OJHMSR JH EVY FWJBPJFCU EVJBA; EVYWYNSWY AYE OJHMSR:

CBM OJEV CUU EVD AYEEJBA AYE ZBMYWHECBMJBA.

FWSKYWXH 4:7   *Clue: J = I*

JONAH'S STORY

KIHNP, CV FV OHOPEPD, FDKF CIPKF SHFM, KOZ SIM KCKHONF HF; BVI FDPHI UHSAPZOPNN HN SVQP LW RPBVIP QP. RLF XVOKD IVNP LW FV BTPP LOFV FKINDHND BIVQ FDP WIPNPOSP VB FDP TVIZ, KOZ UPOF ZVUO FV XVWWK.

XVOKD 1:2–3

Clue: S = C

A SGAYN CZ GYFDRJ RK LAJY FKKTASUARJ BJUR UEY TRGN, FJN EY EYFGN LY; RBU RK UEY CYTTZ RK EYTT SGAYN A, FJN UERB EYFGNYDU LZ ORASY. KRG UERB EFNDU SFDU LY AJUR UEY NYYM, AJ UEY LANDU RK UEY DYFD; FJN UEY KTRRND SRLMFDDYN LY FCRBU.

XRJFE 2:2–3

Clue: C = B

LAMENTABLE

IZC IEBI BIJ MZKS OZUJKJS BIJ SENRIBJK ZD GQZL CQBI E OMZNS QL IQX ELRJK, ELS OEXB SZCL DKZF IJEUJL NLBZ BIJ JEKBI BIJ AJENBW ZD QXKEJM, ELS KJFJFAJKJS LZB IQX DZZBXBZZM QL BIJ SEW ZD IQX ELRJK!

MEFJLBEBQZLX 2:1   *Clue: M = L*

DHA SXC KHAR ENKK PHS VUIS HDD DHA CGCA: LOS SXHOBX XC VUOIC BANCD, JCS ENKK XC XUGC VHZFUIINHP UVVHARNPB SH SXC ZOKSNSORC HD XNI ZCAVNCI.

KUZCPSUSNHPI 3:31–32   *Clue: U = A*

PARABLES OF JESUS

JSH MW DFJQW J FJCJLRW OSAP AMWE, NJS AMW LRYSH RWJH

AMW LRYSH? DMJRR AMWT SPA LPAM VJRR YSAP AMW HYANM?

ROQW 6:39   *Clue: L = B*

ORN HEFDLUS UW RNIKNF EV PEHN OU I DTIEF UW SCVOITL

VNNL, ZREJR I SIF OUUH, IFL VUZNL EF REV WENPL: ZREJR

EFLNNL EV ORN PNIVO UW IPP VNNLV: MCO ZRNF EO EV DTUZF,

EO EV ORN DTNIONVO ISUFD RNTMV, IFL MNJUSNOR I OTNN,

VU ORIO ORN METLV UW ORN IET JUSN IFL PULDN EF ORN

MTIFJRNV ORNTNUW.

SIOORNZ 13:31–32   *Clue: C = U*

MORE PARABLES OF JESUS

RFMGUVA ZRARJYV WZRBV UV CFGM GUVI; GUV BLFHTMI ME

UVROVF LW YLBV CFGM YVROVF, QULDU R QMIRF GMMB, RFT

ULT LF GUAVV IVRWCAVW ME IVRY, GLYY GUV QUMYV QRW

YVROVFVT.

IRGGUVQ 13:33   *Clue: R = A*

WPQ MDYEW Y LYEYAMD PT OID TCJ OEDD; QIDW ICX AEYWBI

CX RDO ODWGDE, YWG LZOODOI TPEOI MDYSDX, RD VWPQ OIYO

XZHHDE CX WCJI: XP MCVDQCXD RD, QIDW RD XIYMM XDD YMM

OIDXD OICWJX, VWPQ OIYO CO CX WDYE, DSDW YO OID GPPEX.

HYOOIDQ 24:32—33   *Clue: M = L*

JEWELRY IN THE BIBLE

BAP MCSU IBGS, VHMC GSA BAP YHGSA, BN

GBAU BN YSTS YEJJEAO CSBTMSP, BAP VTHXOCM VTBISJSMN, BAP

SBTTEAON, BAP TEAON, BAP MBVJSMN, BJJ FSYSJN HL OHJP: BAP

SKSTU GBA MCBM HLLSTSP HLLSTSP BA HLLSTEAO HL OHJP XAMH

MCS JHTP.

SZHPXN 35:22

Clue: Y = W

UO ENDE WDZ ENI RPHW YURR EDMI DYDZ ENI FHDLIHZ PA

ENIUH EUOMRUOQ PHODCIOEG DFPVE ENIUH AIIE...ENI TNDUOG,

DOW ENI FHDTIRIEG, DOW ENI CVAARIHG, ENI FPOOIEG, DOW

ENI PHODCIOEG PA ENI RIQG, DOW ENI NIDWFDOWG, DOW ENI

EDFRIEG, DOW ENI IDHHUOQG, ENI HUOQG, DOW OPGI BIYIRG.

UGDUDN 3:18—21

Clue: F = B

33

OLD FOLKS

LWC KLGDPB KVJDC LAQDE BD XDILQ WNLB AVJD BZWCEDC

WVWDQU LWC AVJD UDLEM, LWC XDILQ MNWM LWC CLZIBQDEM:

LWC LKK QBD CLUM NA KLGDPB ODED MDJDW BZWCEDC

MDJDWQU LWC MDJDW UDLEM: LWC BD CVDC.

IDWDMVM 5:30–31   *Clue: K = L*

GLA ICBEHFCPGE PNSCA GL EHLAOCA CNWEBK GLA FCSCL

KCGOF, GLA TCWGB PGICXE. GLA ICBEHFCPGE PNSCA GQBCO

EC TCWGB PGICXE FCSCL EHLAOCA CNWEBK GLA BDV KCGOF,

GLA TCWGB FVLF GLA AGHWEBCOF: GLA GPP BEC AGKF VQ

ICBEHFCPGE DCOC LNLC EHLAOCA FNZBK GLA LNLC KCGOF: GLA

EC ANCA.

WCLCFNF 5:25–27   *Clue: N = I*

THEOLOGY OF ROMANS, PART 1

COKDKPBDK JA COK LKKLZ BP COK URX COKDK ZORUU VB

PUKZO JK YTZCWPWKL WV OWZ ZWHOC: PBD JA COK URX WZ

COK QVBXUKLHK BP ZWV.

DBERVZ 3:20

Clue: B = O

EBP YIJ SWZSVSQCJ YISWFV BE ISO EPBO YIJ LPJUYSBW BE YIJ

DBPCR UPJ LCJUPCK VJJW, QJSWF MWRJPVYBBR QK YIJ YISWFV

YIUY UPJ OURJ, JZJW ISV JYJPWUC TBDJP UWR FBRIJUR; VB YIUY

YIJK UPJ DSYIBMY JNLMVJ: QJLUMVJ YIUY, DIJW YIJK XWJD FBR,

YIJK FCBPSESJR ISO WBY UV FBR, WJSYIJP DJPJ YIUWXEMC; QMY

QJLUOJ ZUSW SW YIJSP SOUFSWUYSBWV.

PBOUWV 1:20—21

Clue: S = I

THEOLOGY OF ROMANS, PART 2

CEP TC, ONJB OJ OJPJ JBJYTJK, OJ OJPJ PJWEBWTSJI QE UEI

ZH QNJ IJVQN EC NTK KEB, YXWN YEPJ, ZJTBU PJWEBWTSJI, OJ

KNVSS ZJ KVLJI ZH NTK STCJ.

PEYVBK 5:10

Clue: C = F

FLBWB HC FLBWBGJWB RJD RJ NJRZBQROFHJR FJ FLBQ DLHNL

OWB HR NLWHCF ABCYC, DLJ DOIT RJF OGFBW FLB GIBCL, MYF

OGFBW FLB CUHWHF. GJW FLB IOD JG FLB CUHWHF JG IHGB HR

NLWHCF ABCYC LOFL QOZB QB GWBB GWJQ FLB IOD JG CHR

ORZ ZBOFL.

WJQORC 8:1–2

Clue: Z = D

IRD VPJ IWGJ RN VPJ GWI DWY IWCWE; WIS VPJ IWGJ RN PTY

DTNJ WCTXWTE: WIS YPJ DWY W DRGWI RN XRRS AISJZYVWISTIX,

WIS RN W CJWAVTNAE FRAIVJIWIFJ: CAV VPJ GWI DWY FPAZETYP

WIS JBTE TI PTY SRTIXY; WIS PJ DWY RN VPJ PRAYJ RN FWEJC.

1 YWGAJE 25:3

Clue: P = H

CALP AFD SJCALH JPZ AFD ERCALH DJFZ BPCR AFE, FD CALHL

PLGLH J IREJP JERPV CAL ZJBVACLHD RS CAQ OHLCAHLP, RH

JERPV JXX EQ MLRMXL, CAJC CARB VRLDC CR CJYL J IFSL RS

CAL BPWFHWBEWFDLZ MAFXFDCFPLD? JPZ DJEDRP DJFZ BPCR

AFD SJCALH, VLC ALH SRH EL; SRH DAL MXLJDLCA EL ILXX.

TBZVLD 14:3

Clue: S = F

GOSPEL VILLAIN

LWUA UALUOUI VFLFA CALJ MPIFV VPOAFHUI CVBFOCJL, QUCAD

JG LWU APHQUO JG LWU LTURYU. FAI WU TUAL WCV TFK, FAI

BJHHPAUI TCLW LWU BWCUG EOCUVLV FAI BFELFCAV, WJT WU

HCDWL QULOFK WCH PALJ LWUH.

RPSU 22:3–4   *Clue: V = S*

MPBCOR, C SPZY MCOOYH CO ASPA C SPZY VYAIPBYH ASY

COONGYOA VUNNH. POH ASYB MPCH, LSPA CM ASPA AN EM?

MYY ASNE AN ASPA. POH SY GPMA HNLO ASY WCYGYM NX

MCUZYI CO ASY AYDWUY, POH HYWPIAYH, POH LYOA POH

SPORYH SCDMYUX.

DPAASYL 27:4–5   *Clue: G = C*

THOUGHTS FOR PHILEMON

C UERV GEDK IJCNNKO CN ICNG ACOK WIO GEOP, C ICVV JKUEZ

CN: EVTKCN C PW OWN YEZ NW NGKK GWI NGWR WIKYN RONW

AK KDKO NGCOK WIO YKVB TKYCPKY.

UGCVKAWO 19

Clue: Y = S

K OVRGL FE UTH, FRLKGU FYGOKTG TP OVYY RIAREN KG FE

XWREYWN, VYRWKGU TP OVE ITCY RGH PRKOV, AVKMV OVTD

VRNO OTARWH OVY ITWH BYNDN, RGH OTARWH RII NRKGON;

OVRO OVY MTFFDGKMROKTG TP OVE PRKOV FRE QYMTFY

YPPYMODRI QE OVY RMLGTAIYHUKGU TP YCYWE UTTH OVKGU

AVKMV KN KG ETD KG MVWKNO BYNDN.

XVKIYFTG 4–6

Clue: A = W

GOATS IN THE BIBLE

JN FA RFY YFH, CRFBR RL RWMR YFHHLE, BJVL MJ RFY

GHJCILESL: MRLH RL YRWII ONFHS RFY JAALNFHS, W GFE JA MRL

SJWMY, W ALVWIL CFMRJPM OILVFYR, AJN RFY YFH CRFBR RL

RWMR YFHHLE.

ILXFMFBPY 4:28   *Clue: M = T*

INSR MOKJ ILLQ INFSS INLKMORC WNLMSR TSR LKI LZ OJJ

VMFOSJ, ORC BSRI IL MSSQ COEVC ORC NVM TSR KXLR INS

FLWQM LZ INS BVJC PLOIM.

1 MOTKSJ 24:2   *Clue: C = D*

UIK OGK MUWK, NTH HPTLT RT NWOPHM WI HPT BWLEUETIH GB HPT

PTUZTI HG KWZWKT HPT KUQ BLGE HPT IWOPH; UIK NTH HPTE RT

BGL MWOIM, UIK BGL MTUMGIM, UIK BGL KUQM, UIK QTULM: UIK NTH

HPTE RT BGL NWOPHM WI HPT BWLEUETIH GB HPT PTUZTI HG OWZT

NWOPH VFGI HPT TULHP: UIK WH SUM MG.

OTITMWM 1:14–15   *Clue: B = F*

TRP LSP HVOTDOP LVOTD ZXTBOJ, TRP ONOVC BANARL

HVOTDMVO DXTD YSNODX, ZXAHX DXO ZTDOVJ IVSMLXD WSVDX

TIMRPTRDBC, TWDOV DXOAV UARP, TRP ONOVC ZARLOP WSZB

TWDOV XAJ UARP: TRP LSP JTZ DXTD AD ZTJ LSSP. TRP LSP

IBOJJOP DXOY, JTCARL, IO WVMADWMB, TRP YMBDAFBC.

LOROJAJ 1:21–22   *Clue: L = G*

CITIES IN ACTS

NGU N DFOCNJG SBING GNIFU RXUJN, N TFRRFO BE LPOLRF, BE

CWF DJCX BE CWXNCJON, SWJDW SBOTWJLLFU ABU, WFNOU PT:

SWBTF WFNOC CWF RBOU BLFGFU, CWNC TWF NCCFGUFU PGCB

CWF CWJGAT SWJDW SFOF TLBVFG BE LNPR.

NDCT 16:14

Clue: U = D

FPQ VTW SLWVTLWP JCCWQJFVWIX NWPV FEFX HFOI FPQ NJIFN

SX PJKTV OPVD SWLWF: ETD RDCJPK VTJVTWL EWPV JPVD VTW

NXPFKDKOW DZ VTW GWEN.

FRVN 17:10

Clue: E = W

OLD TESTAMENT MOTHERS

CQLSLMNSL BJ TGFL JN RGAA, CQLD JQL JBFL CGA TNFL GONYJ GMJLS QGDDGQ QGI TNDTLBELI, JQGJ AQL OGSL G AND, GDI TGKKLI QBA DGFL AGFYLK, AGUBDP, OLTGYAL B QGEL GAWLI QBF NM JQL KNSI.

1 AGFYLK 1:20

Clue: O = B

EHZ KEOEP XEPA EXPEV E RDH: EHZ EXPEV JEYYAZ KGR RDH'R HEVA, UKGJK KEOEP XEPA, GRKVEAY.

OAHARGR 16:15

Clue: V = M

MORE OLD TESTAMENT MOTHERS

QGA BSASI JGLJURDUP, SLP WSAU SWASISC S BGL RL IRB GEP

SNU, SM MIU BUM MRCU GQ FIRJI NGP ISP BHGVUL MG IRC.

NULUBRB 21:2

Clue: I = H

GL HLTQ KLLX NCKY, TRI GYO UTG YWG UWSO: TRI UYOR YO

UORK WR CRKL YON, KYO ZLNI PTJO YON ALRAODKWLR, TRI GYO

HTNO T GLR.

NCKY 4:13

Clue: W = I

JESUS' WORDS TO THE CHURCHES

WN QRDI ZDHPMWD QRNM PGQ OMCDTPGB, PIK IDAQRDG HNOK

ING RNQ, A TAOO WEMD QRDD NMQ NX BJ BNMQR.

GDUDOPQANI 3:16

Clue: O = L

AN ZAHZ MPNFGMKNZA, ZAN IHKN IAHOO DN GOMZANR UE

BAUZN FHUKNEZ; HER U BUOO EMZ DOMZ MCZ AUI EHKN MCZ

MT ZAN DMMQ MT OUTN, DCZ U BUOO GMETNII AUI EHKN

DNTMFN KX THZANF, HER DNTMFN AUI HEYNOI.

FNPNOHZUME 3:5

Clue: T = F

ANIMALS OF THE BIBLE

VWVTI RBTVV IVNTF CUGV GNPV RBV FBSMF CE RNTFBSFB

HTSUJSUJ JCYL, NUL FSYWVT, SWCTI, NUL NMVF, NUL MVNGCGOF.

2 GBTCUSGYVF 9:21   *Clue: S = I*

KYV PLEX FEUL UYFEE NPVEE PDKY KYV EFSW, FCN KYV EVLJFON

UYFEE EDV NLPC PDKY KYV HDN;

FCN KYV QFEX FCN KYV TLZCB EDLC FCN KYV XFKEDCB

KLBVKYVO; FCN F EDKKEV QYDEN UYFEE EVFN KYVS.

DUFDFY 11:6   *Clue: L = O*

MIRACLES OF PAUL

CGL DYL SKYVDWO AUTFECP NEKCFPTA HQ OWT WCGLA YB

UCVP: AY OWCO BKYN WEA HYLQ STKT HKYVDWO VGOY OWT AEFI

WCGLITKFWETBA YK CUKYGA, CGL OWT LEATCATA LTUCKOTL BKYN

OWTN, CGL OWT TREP AUEKEOA STGO YVO YB OWTN.

CFOA 19:11–12   *Clue: V = U*

BAK DS NBEI SR YBHH, SMBS SMI TBSMIG RT YJOZDJH ZBL HDNP

RT B TIXIG BAK RT B OZRRKL TZJQ: SR FMRE YBJZ IASIGIK DA,

BAK YGBLIK, BAK ZBDK MDH MBAKH RA MDE, BAK MIBZIK MDE.

BNSH 28:8   *Clue: Y = P*

PROVERBALLY SPEAKING, PART 1

MQVY MBHZRJ VYWVAVWQ BYWR WQBYV QVNAW, NYZ

CYRMOVZIV BH GOVNHNYW DYWR WQK HRDO; ZBHFAVWBRY

HQNOO GAVHVASV WQVV, DYZVAHWNYZBYI HQNOO CVVG WQVV.

GARSVAUH 2:10–11   *Clue: O = L*

CRU PWUKKBGZ NJ CRU WNLI, BC HTAUCR LBSR, TGI RU TIIUCR

GN KNLLND DBCR BC.

FLNEULPK 10:22   *Clue: N = O*

PROVERBALLY SPEAKING, PART 2

NVY UGHN MAOOAS DK DO OV XAO YDKWVU ONPJ XVBW! PJW

OV XAO GJWASKOPJWDJX SPONAS OV MA HNVKAJ ONPJ KDBIAS!

ZSVIASMK 16:16   *Clue: K = S*

UTEK PS DBOKPWLZOI XOCZ TP TPABM UTP; TPW XOCZ T

DNBOSNL UTP CZSN LZTRC PSC AS: RKLC CZSN RKTBP ZOL XTML,

TPW AKC T LPTBK CS CZM LSNR.

IBSGKBJL 22:24–25   *Clue: R = L*

49

EX-QUEENS

HOU LRM IAOD EVPMU MWLRMY HQVPM HEE LRM TVGMO, HOU
WRM VQLHAOMU DYHJM HOU KHPVCY AO RAW WADRL GVYM
LRHO HEE LRM PAYDAOW; WV LRHL RM WML LRM YVNHE JYVTO
CZVO RMY RMHU, HOU GHUM RMY FCMMO AOWLMHU VK
PHWRLA.

MWLRMY 2:17

Clue: E = L

YMAUAECUA KMAZ NSJA SPSFO, SOI KCDI MFJ. SOI MA BSFI, KMFB
FB KMA YCUI CE KMA DCUI, YMFNM MA BVSRA GZ MFB BAUXSOK
ADFLSM KMA KFBMGFKA, BSZFOP, FO KMA VCUKFCO CE LAHUAAD
BMSDD ICPB ASK KMA EDABM CE LAHAGAD.

2 RFOPB 9:36

Clue: L = J

A NOTE FROM JUDE

PBOLEBW, HIBY T JKEB KOO WTOTJBYDB SL HCTSB AYSL ULA LQ

SIB DLVVLY MKOEKSTLY, TS HKM YBBWQAO QLC VB SL HCTSB

AYSL ULA, KYW BNILCS ULA SIKS UB MILAOW BKCYBMSOU

DLYSBYW QLC SIB QKTSI HITDI HKM LYDB WBOTEBCBW AYSL SIB

MKTYSM.

XAWB 3   *Clue: A = U*

JGF YJWG ZLT WZXW LA XNUO WG IOOS QGY PMGT PXUULJR,

XJE WG SMOAOJW QGY PXYUWUOAA NOPGMO WZO SMOAOJVO

GP ZLA RUGMQ FLWZ OBVOOELJR CGQ, WG WZO GJUQ FLAO

RGE GYM AXDLGYM, NO RUGMQ XJE TXCOAWQ, EGTLJLGJ XJE

SGFOM.

CYEO 24–25   *Clue: N = B*

EZEKIEL'S VISIONS

NKB KOUP EV NKB IEFP GOR CZEU AB, OUP MOFFYBP AB ECN YU

NKB RZYFYN EV NKB IEFP, OUP RBN AB PEGU YU NKB AYPRN EV

NKB LOIIBH GKYMK GOR VCII EV XEUBR.

BQBJYBI 37:1

Clue: P = D

IBS O WTTVMS, IBS, UMYTWS, I JYOKWJOBS ZILM TEC TH CYM BTKCY, I

PKMIC ZWTES, IBS I HOKM OBHTWSOBP OCNMWH, IBS I UKOPYCBMNN

JIN IUTEC OC, IBS TEC TH CYM LOSNC CYMKMTH IN CYM ZTWTEK TH

ILUMK, TEC TH CYM LOSNC TH CYM HOKM. IWNT TEC TH CYM LOSNC

CYMKMTH ZILM CYM WOVMBMNN TH HTEK WOROBP ZKMICEKMN. IBS

CYON JIN CYMOK IXXMIKIBZM; CYMG YIS CYM WOVMBMNN TH I LIB.

MAMVOMW 1:4–5

Clue: Z = C

ON THE MENU

DYF EUNY GUN XUMIFKNY PC MLKDNI LDE MG, GUNW LDMF PYN

GP DYPGUNK, MG ML TDYYD: CPK GUNW EMLG YPG EUDG MG

EDL. DYF TPLNL LDMF VYGP GUNT, GUML ML GUN RKNDF EUMXU

GUN IPKF UDGU BMONY WPV GP NDG.

NHPFVL 16:15   *Clue: E = W*

HCG BDFC XHA IEDVFYG XKVF IHJYE'A FHKP, HCG XKVF H

WKPGEY DU H AOKC HTDNV FKA EDKCA; HCG FY GKG YHV

EDINAVA HCG XKEG FDCYR.

JHPO 1:6   *Clue: I = C*

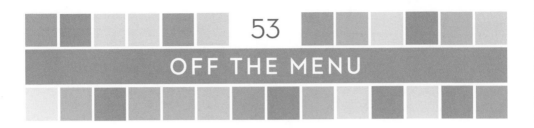

PT WVGZZ JCD TGD CE GJPDVAJI DVGD SATDV CE ADWTZE: DVCL

WVGZD IART AD LJDC DVT WDQGJITQ DVGD AW AJ DVP IGDTW,

DVGD VT BGP TGD AD.

STLDTQCJCBP 14:21   *Clue: J = N*

RMO BEH DSTMH, BEFZJE EH OTGTOH BEH EFFK, RMO QH

NWFGHMKFFBHO, PHB EH NEHSHBE MFB BEH NZO; EH TD

ZMNWHRM BF PFZ.

WHGTBTNZD 11:7   *Clue: N = C*

MODES OF TRANSPORTATION

FWKK MW FYW EICSYFWL JA UTJR, XWYJKE, FYM HTRS GJVWFY

CRFJ FYWW, VWWH, IRE UTFFTRS COJR IR IUU, IRE I GJKF FYW

AJIK JA IR IUU.

VIFFYWN 21:5   *Clue: E = D*

BAF UDKTYM OBFT ITBFC MJK PMBIJDL, BAF VTAL XY LD OTTL

JKIBTH MJK EBLMTI, LD QDKMTA, BAF YITKTALTF MJOKTHE XALD

MJO; BAF MT ETHH DA MJK ATPZ, BAF VTYL DA MJK ATPZ B

QDDF VMJHT.

QTATKJK 46:29   *Clue: V = W*

2 CORINTHIANS

IRAMG IG MYYZ CYS NS SRG SRACPQ IRAKR NWG QGGC, UDS NS

SRG SRACPQ IRAKR NWG CYS QGGC: VYW SRG SRACPQ IRAKR

NWG QGGC NWG SGOEYWNM; UDS SRG SRACPQ IRAKR NWG CYS

QGGC NWG GSGWCNM.

2 KYWACSRANCQ 4:18   *Clue: Y = O*

PVCYDTP SHGFBPJLPB, QOPMOPF SP UP DT MOP KCDMO; IFHLP

SHGF HQT BPJLPB. ETHQ SP THM SHGF HQT BPJLPB, OHQ MOCM

XPBGB NOFDBM DB DT SHG, PVNPIM SP UP FPIFHUCMPB?

2 NHFDTMODCTB 13:5   *Clue: U = B*

THE NUMBER OF PERFECTION

BOZ NEZ IHYAAYZ URY AYSYOUR ZBP, BOZ ABOQUCMCYZ CU:

IYQBLAY URBU CO CU RY RBZ VYAUYZ MVEF BHH RCA XEVW

XRCQR NEZ QVYBUYZ BOZ FBZY.

NYOYACA 2:3   *Clue: R = H*

JFY WPRHR BJVR DFWC VR CFR CI WPR ORXRF JFSRGO QPMBP

PJY WPR ORXRF XMJGO IDGG CI WPR ORXRF GJOW EGJSDRO,

JFY WJGARY QMWP VR, OJTMFS, BCVR PMWPRH, M QMGG OPRQ

WPRR WPR ZHMYR, WPR GJVZ'O QMIR.

HRXRGJWMCF 21:9   *Clue: Z = B*

CAE LOT PJWE GCFE MALJ GCLCA, OCGL LOJM YJAGFETWTE ZK

GTWBCAL NJH, LOCL LOTWT FG AJAT PFIT OFZ FA LOT TCWLO, C

DTWUTYL CAE CA MDWFXOL ZCA, JAT LOCL UTCWTLO XJE, CAE

TGYOTQTLO TBFP?

NJH 1:8   *Clue: M = U*

WKRT ACWCT CTADRBRM WKR XSBM, CTM ACJM, MSWK ESO

HRCB VSM HSB TSGVKW? KCAW TSW WKSG UCMR CT KRMVR

COSGW KJU, CTM COSGW KJA KSGAR, CTM COSGW CXX WKCW

KR KCWK ST RYRBL AJMR?

ESO 1:9—10   *Clue: A = S*

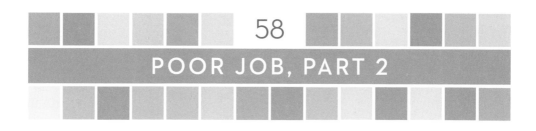
POOR JOB, PART 2

TE RUMO TWR CEBY BKRU UKS AQEY RUM

JFEAYC TMNMY CWOT WYC TMNMY YKJURT, WYC YEYM TQWXM

W BEFC AYRE UKS: VEF RUMO TWB RUWR UKT JFKMV BWT NMFO

JFMWR.

GEI 2:13   *Clue: J = G*

GOMU YNC WPNHM, WUE PMUG ODH VWUGBM, WUE

HOWLME ODH OMWE, WUE KMBB ENSU IZNU GOM XPNIUE,

WUE SNPHODZZME, WUE HWDE, UWJME RWVM D NIG NK VT

VNGOMP'H SNVC, WUE UWJME HOWBB D PMGIPU GODGOMP:

GOM BNPE XWLM, WUE GOM BNPE OWGO GWJMU WSWT.

YNC 1:20—21   *Clue: V = M*

JOB RESTORED

AUKT SYW ETRVKIKO AUK XYIO, ETO REHO, H

DTYV AUEA AUYZ NETRA OY KGKIF AUHTJ, ETO AUEA TY AUYZJUA

NET WK VHAUUYXOKT LIYQ AUKK.

SYW 42:1–2   *Clue: H = I*

LR HUS KRME VKSLLSE HUS KFHHSM SYE RA GRV ZRMS HUFY

UBL VSJBYYBYJ: ARM US UFE ARQMHSSY HURQLFYE LUSSD, FYE

LBC HURQLFYE NFZSKL, FYE F HURQLFYE WRTS RA RCSY, FYE

F HURQLFYE LUS FLLSL. US UFE FKLR LSXSY LRYL LRYL FYE HUMSS

EFQJUHSML.

GRV 42:12–13   *Clue: V = B*

LAS ZPRA KPRU ZRCR DIWR KI KPR FTLDR, ZPGDP GY DLTTRS

DLTJLCU, KPRCR KPRU DCEDGBGRS PGW, LAS KPR WLTRBLDKICY,

IAR IA KPR CGNPK PLAS, LAS KPR IKPRC IA KPR TRBK.

TEHR 23:33   *Clue: Z = W*

HVU HQOFM OPHO OPFL PHU BSRCFU PYB, OPFL OSSC OPF

MSXF SQQ QMSB PYB, HVU GZO PYJ SEV MHYBFVO SV PYB, HVU

IFU PYB HEHL OS RMZRYQL PYB. HVU HJ OPFL RHBF SZO, OPFL

QSZVU H BHV SQ RLMFVF, JYBSV XL VHBF: PYB OPFL RSBGFIIFU

OS XFHM PYJ RMSJJ.

BHOOPFE 27:31–32   *Clue: R = C*

GIDEON

STBUPJ, F EFPP VXC H WPTTAT UW EUUP FR CBT WPUUI; HRJ

FW CBT JTE ST UR CBT WPTTAT URPN, HRJ FC ST JIN XVUR HPP

CBT THICB STYFJT, CBTR YBHPP F QRUE CBHC CBUX EFPC YHGT

FYIHTP SN DFRT BHRJ, HY CBUX BHYC YHFJ.

OXJZTY 6:37

Clue: S = B

EKY CFI CFQII WTADEKSIJ LRIB CFI CQGADICJ, EKY LQEXI CFI

DSCWFIQJ, EKY FIRY CFI READJ SK CFISQ RINC FEKYJ, EKY CFI

CQGADICJ SK CFISQ QSZFC FEKYJ CT LRTB BSCFER: EKY CFIV

WQSIY, CFI JBTQY TN CFI RTQY, EKY TN ZSYITK.

MGYZIJ 7:20

Clue: B = W

TEMPTATION

FWIBI WYFW HN FIUZFYFLNH FYMIH SNV PVF EVOW YE LE

ONUUNH FN UYH: PVF ANR LE KYLFWKVX, CWN CLXX HNF

EVKKIB SNV FN PI FIUZFIR YPNDI FWYF SI YBI YPXI; PVF CLXX

CLFW FWI FIUZFYFLNH YXEN UYMI Y CYS FN IEOYZI, FWYF SI UYS

PI YPXI FN PIYB LF.

1 ONBLHFWLYHE 10:13   *Clue: K = F*

ZT REZTL, ZT CYWYJXGH; ZTAXQRT BEQL XFCTLRXLB HMT FTCYJ,

XR X LEXLYGW JYEG, KXJPTHM XZEQH, RTTPYGW KMED MT DXB

FTCEQL: KMED LTRYRH RHTFUXRH YG HMT UXYHM.

1 VTHTL 5:8–9   *Clue: F = D*

FRAMED

JWL JPJN IJRF BWCA PBK PAEKF PFJUD JWL LBKVMFJKFL NFIJEKF

AZ CPF TAXL TPBIP WJNACP CPF GFYXFFMBCF PJL KVAQFW CA PBR:

ZAX PF PJL KJBL, B TBMM WAC HBUF CPFF CPF BWPFXBCJWIF AZ RD

ZJCPFXK.... NEC GFYFNFM PBK TBZF IJRF CA PBR, JWL KJBL EWCA

PBR, TPD BK CPD KVBXBC KA KJL, CPJC CPAE FJCFKC WA NXFJL?

1 QBWHK 21:4–5   *Clue: I = C*

XCEAOUPZ U GUVW, UJI VLW JUSEWY EJ YPDY UZEJD WYL

XLEXOL: UJI VLW WKE ZLJ, VEJV EG SLOPUO, SLGECL YPZ, WE

SLUC KPWJLVV UDUPJVW YPZ, VUHPJD, WYEB IPIVW SOUVXYLZL

DEI UJI WYL RPJD. UJI WYLJ AUCCH YPZ EBW, UJI VWEJL YPZ.

1 RPJDV 21:9–10   *Clue: O = L*

PROTECTING MARRIAGE

KJFBW LHORJN GCO GE OYFBR GLB QFNORJB, HBK JCBBFBP

LHORJN GCO GE OYFBR GLB LRDD.

UJGTRJIN 5:15

Clue: F = I

FAO ONQ GECXOJWX VA VFADDAL: JXL TABEWUA KWON ONA

KWGA EG ONQ QECON. FAO NAT VA JD ONA FEZWXS NWXL

JXL IFAJDJXO TEA; FAO NAT VTAJDOD DJOWDGQ ONAA JO JFF

OWHAD; JXL VA ONEC TJZWDNAL JFKJQD KWON NAT FEZA.

ITEZATVD 5:18–19

Clue: L = D

FROM THE BOOK OF GALATIANS

TWGEZP WHPW GSKSSYSK AZ CGDY PWS TAGZS DC PWS JHO,

VSEBX YHKS H TAGZS CDG AZ: CDG EP EZ OGEPPSB, TAGZSK EZ

SRSGN DBS PWHP WHBXSPW DB H PGSS.

XHJHPEHBZ 3:13

Clue: E = I

FAYTEAB NCMN M KMA EV AYN WPVNEIEGJ LQ NCG TYHFV YI

NCG UMT, LPN LQ NCG IMENC YI WGVPV ZCHEVN, GOGA TG

CMOG LGUEGOGJ EA WGVPV ZCHEVN, NCMN TG KEBCN LG

WPVNEIEGJ LQ NCG IMENC YI ZCHEVN, MAJ AYN LQ NCG TYHFV

YI NCG UMT: IYH LQ NCG TYHFV YI NCG UMT VCMUU AY IUGVC

LG WPVNEIEGJ.

BMUMNEMAV 2:16

Clue: F = K

SNAKES IN THE BIBLE

BMOWOCFWO BMO ROFRHO UYSO BF SFAOA, YIP AYXP, GO

MYNO AXIIOP, CFW GO MYNO ARFJOI YEYXIAB BMO HFWP, YIP

YEYXIAB BMOO; RWYQ VIBF BMO HFWP, BMYB MO BYJO YGYQ

BMO AOWROIBA CWFS VA. YIP SFAOA RWYQOP CFW BMO

ROFRHO.

IVSZOWA 21:7   *Clue: R = P*

UIC FBKI LUOT BUC DUABKYKC U POICTK QN ZAGHEZ, UIC TUGC

ABKS QI ABK NGYK, ABKYK HUSK U JGLKY QOA QN ABK BKUA,

UIC NUZAKIKC QI BGZ BUIC.

UHAZ 28:3   *Clue: T = L*

TRUE BEAUTY

UPL OTG VAGB T QASNELEI ULYTG? VLS PFS MSAOF AI VTS TDLQF

SEDAFI. NPF PFTSN LV PFS PEIDTGB BLNP ITVFCZ NSEIN AG PFS,

IL NPTN PF IPTCC PTQF GL GFFB LV IMLAC.

MSLQFSDI 31:10–11   *Clue: E = U*

NDWXB YLWICHCM RBU HU CWU TB UDYU WSUNYIL YLWICHCM

WJ QRYHUHCM UDB DYHI, YCL WJ NBYIHCM WJ MWRL, WI WJ

QSUUHCM WC WJ YQQYIBR; TSU RBU HU TB UDB DHLLBC AYC WJ

UDB DBYIU, HC UDYU NDHKD HX CWU KWIISQUHTRB, BGBC

UDB WICYABCU WJ Y ABBP YCL OSHBU XQHIHU.

1 QBUBI 3:3–4   *Clue: Q = P*

68

A LITTLE R & R

IAL XCLLM FQ O COVFWKZUE POU ZX XDLLI, DALIALK AL LOI

CZIICL FK PWNA: VWI IAL OVWUHOUNL FQ IAL KZNA DZCC UFI

XWQQLK AZP IF XCLLM.

LNNCLXZOXILX 5:12   *Clue: X = S*

UEY GK NUMY HEBL BGKQ, ILQK SK SLHONKCXKN UDUOB MEBL

U YKNKOB DCUIK, UEY OKNB U FGMCK: ZLO BGKOK FKOK QUES

ILQMEA UEY ALMEA, UEY BGKS GUY EL CKMNHOK NL QHIG UN

BL KUB.

QUOV 6:31   *Clue: Q = M*

QUOTABLE EXODUS

C TY VLS GRFH VLA DRH, JLCPL LTES IFRNDLV VLSS RNV RM VLS GTZH RM SDAXV, RNV RM VLS LRNWS RM IRZHTDS. VLRN WLTGV LTES ZR RVLSF DRHW ISMRFS YS.

SQRHNW 20:2–3

Clue: D = G

NVU TY ANRU, R CRII ONFY NII OJ XLLUVYAA SNAA PYQLKY ETYY, NVU R CRII SKLBINRO ETY VNOY LQ ETY ILKU PYQLKY ETYY; NVU CRII PY XKNBRLWA EL CTLO R CRII PY XKNBRLWA, NVU CRII ATYC OYKBJ LV CTLO R CRII ATYC OYKBJ.

YZLUWA 33:19

Clue: P = B

FRIENDS OF JESUS

CFV DOLXL KFJON ZEPASE, ECN SOP LTLAOP, ECN KEREPXL.

VSOC SO SEN SOEPN ASOPOIFPO ASEA SO VEL LTBH, SO EWFNO

AVF NEQL LATKK TC ASO LEZO YKEBO VSOPO SO VEL.

DFSC 11:5–6   *Clue: L = S*

HSV HD WAV WFH FALGA AVJUO QHAS NBVJY, JSO DHCCHFVO

ALT, FJN JSOUVF, NLTHS BVWVU'N PUHWAVU. AV DLUNW DLSOVWA

ALN HFS PUHWAVU NLTHS, JSO NJLWA KSWH ALT, FV AJXV DHKSO

WAV TVNNLJN, FALGA LN, PVLSE LSWVUBUVWVO, WAV GAULNW.

QHAS 1:40–41   *Clue: G = C*

ANIMAL MIRACLES

BQP DES WMGP MCSQSP DES NMRDE MT DES BII, BQP IES IBJP

RQDM OBWBBN, LEBD EBZS J PMQS RQDM DESS, DEBD DEMR

EBID INJDDSQ NS DESIS DEGSS DJNSI?

QRNOSGI 22:28   *Clue: J = I*

OHERCEYAEIOMCOU, WDAE RD AYHJWM HBBDOM EYDS,

UH EYHJ EH EYD ADI, IOM QIAE IO YHHV,

IOM EIVD JZ EYD BCAY EYIE BCXAE QHSDEY JZ; IOM RYDO

EYHJ YIAE HZDODM YCA SHJEY, EYHJ AYIWE BCOM I ZCDQD HB

SHODK: EYIE EIVD, IOM UCND JOEH EYDS BHX SD IOM EYDD.

SIEEYDR 17:27   *Clue: U = G*

SECRETARIES

WSMX KMTMJNDS RDUUMI LDTBRS WSM GAX AY XMTNDS: DXI

LDTBRS ETAWM YTAJ WSM JABWS AY KMTMJNDS DUU WSM EATIG

AY WSM UATI, ESNRS SM SDI GCAQMX BXWA SNJ, BCAX D TAUU

AY D LAAQ.

KMTMJNDS 36:4

Clue: J = M

D BCGBDSR, AMI AGIBC BMDR CTDRBOC, RWOSBC XIS DF BMC

OIGQ.

GIKWFR 16:22

Clue: O = L

KSOPS DNQRJS NVPJBVBC, GVOGL, NLA YTRONARC, NLA JSR

PSNDFRVC GE JSR CGBJS. KSOPS AGRJS XVRNJ JSOLXC YNCJ

EOLAOLX GBJ; MRN, NLA KGLARVC KOJSGBJ LBDFRV.

ZGF 9:9—10   *Clue: O = I*

CSMTMOYTM GKTFLI CSMTM MBML YO YLM, FLR SDA FG IYYR FG

RMFR, GY AFLZ FG CSM GCFTG YO CSM GVZ DL ANXCDCNRM, FLR FG

CSM GFLR ESDHS DG PZ CSM GMF GSYTM DLLNAMTFPXM.

SMPTMEG 11:12   *Clue: R = D*

FIRST CHRISTMAS

WAG JZZ LRNH GJH BAWP, LRJL NL FNVRL OP MXZMNZZPB

GRNQR GJH HIAYPW AM LRP ZAKB OT LRP IKAIRPL, HJTNWV,

OPRAZB, J CNKVNW HRJZZ OP GNLR QRNZB, JWB HRJZZ OKNWV

MAKLR J HAW, JWB LRPT HRJZZ QJZZ RNH WJFP PFFJWXPZ.

FJLLRPG 1:22–23   *Clue: V = G*

SXQ IH UE CSI, ETSE, CTUZF ETFJ CFGF ETFGF, ETF QSJI CFGF

SKKHALZUITFQ ETSE ITF ITHRZQ OF QFZUNFGFQ. SXQ ITF

OGHRMTE VHGET TFG VUGIEOHGX IHX, SXQ CGSLLFQ TUA UX

ICSQQZUXM KZHETFI, SXQ ZSUQ TUA UX S ASXMFG; OFKSRIF

ETFGF CSI XH GHHA VHG ETFA UX ETF UXX.

ZRWF 2:6–7   *Clue: Z = L*

KM KR PT IN, NOW ANF UCNL UT ITWQT KI ZPST RN FTSKQTW OI

MWNL RCT POWEKEA MKTWB MOWEZHT, ZEF CT UKSS FTSKQTW OI

NOR NM RCKET CZEF, N GKEA. POR KM ENR, PT KR GENUE OERN

RCTT, N GKEA, RCZR UT UKSS ENR ITWQT RCB ANFI, ENW UNWICKX

RCT ANSFTE KLZAT UCKHC RCNO CZIR ITR OX.

FZEKTS 3:17–18   *Clue: U = W*

HGT WSJ OQUGMJI, NEZJQGEQI, HGT WSJ MHOWHUGI, HGT WSJ

LUGN'I MEPGIJRREQI, AJUGN NHWSJQJT WENJWSJQ, IHK WSJIJ

VJG, POEG KSEIJ AETUJI WSJ BUQJ SHT GE OEKJQ, GEQ KHI HG

SHUQ EB WSJUQ SJHT IUGNJT, GJUWSJQ KJQJ WSJUQ MEHWI

MSHGNJT, GEQ WSJ IVJRR EB BUQJ SHT OHIIJT EG WSJV.

THGUJR 3:27   *Clue: M = C*

RJAKGB MKD RJAJWKIA, DALVA L WFBJ DLIA IAJJ; AJ JFIJIA TCFUU FU FM KS.

NKR 40:15   *Clue: K = O*

DW MXTM FTZ MXL SCUF PDMX XDO OCUL TWF HULTM TWF OMUCWH OPCUF OXTSS JYWDOX SLQDTMXTW MXL JDLUKDWH OLUJLWM, LQLW SLQDTMXTW MXTM KUCCRLF OLUJLWM; TWF XL OXTSS OSTZ MXL FUTHCW MXTM DO DW MXL OLT.

DOTDTX 27:1   *Clue: J = P*

HMO LJAE YLLADXE OANLDTEAO HXX LJHL GHN RM LJA PRLE,

VTLJ ZHM HMO GTZHM, ETYMI HMO TXO, HMO TK, HMO NJAAC,

HMO HNN, GRLJ LJA AOIA TU LJA NGTDO.

STNJYH 6:21

Clue: L = T

GKS CF HWGUU ABQL FB XGHH, FWGF PWLK FWLM QGIL G UBKY

TUGHF PCFW FWL EGQ'H WBEK, GKS PWLK ML WLGE FWL HBNKS

BZ FWL FENQXLF, GUU FWL XLBXUL HWGUU HWBNF PCFW G

YELGF HWBNF; GKS FWL PGUU BZ FWL ACFM HWGUU ZGUU

SBPK ZUGF, GKS FWL XLBXUL HWGUU GHALKS NX LJLEM QGK

HFEGCYWF TLZBEL WCQ.

RBHWNG 6:5

Clue: Q = M

HOSEA

VSJY DWOU VSJ KAMU PYVA TJ, HA IJV, KAGJ W RATWY NJKAGJU

AC SJM CMOJYU, IJV WY WUPKVJMJDD, WLLAMUOYH VA VSJ

KAGJ AC VSJ KAMU VARWMU VSJ LSOKUMJY AC ODMWJK, RSA

KAAX VA AVSJM HAUD, WYU KAGJ CKWHAYD AC ROYJ.

SADJW 3:1   *Clue: S = H*

C OCWW KJMW VKJCA XMENBWCRCGI, C OCWW WDPJ VKJS

HAJJWZ: HDA SCGJ MGIJA CB VLAGJR MOMZ HADS KCS. C

OCWW XJ MB VKJ RJO LGVD CBAMJW: KJ BKMWW IADO MB VKJ

WCWZ, MGR EMBV HDAVK KCB ADDVB MB WJXMGDG.

KDBJM 14:4–5   *Clue: D = O*

MONEY, MONEY, MONEY

LPW LEJLMLN MSLJZSPSW OPBI SVMJIP; LPW LEJLMLN YSTQMSW

BI SVMJIP BMS FTUXSJ, YMTHM MS MLW PLNSW TP BMS

LOWTSPHS IR BMS FIPF IR MSBM, RIOJ MOPWJSW FMSZSUF IR

FTUXSJ, HOJJSPB NIPSC YTBM BMS NSJHMLPB.

QSPSFTF 23:16   *Clue: T = I*

FRL CDABA AFH QWDE FVFGRAH HSD HEDFABEZ, FRL XDSDNL

SQM HSD UDQUND KFAH YQRDZ GRHQ HSD HEDFABEZ: FRL YFRZ

HSFH MDED EGKS KFAH GR YBKS. FRL HSDED KFYD F KDEHFGR

UQQE MGLQM, FRL ASD HSEDM GR HMQ YGHDA, MSGKS YFID F

JFEHSGRV.

YFEI 12:41–42   *Clue: K = C*

GET SAVED!

KRF GBWA WAS ASNFW VNL JSMBSESWA CLWR FBZAWSRCTLSTT;

NLH GBWA WAS VRCWA PRLKSTTBRL BT VNHS CLWR TNMENWBRL.

FRVNLT 10:10   *Clue: F = R*

EMJWJODWJ, IA FJPDSJC, KV AJ MKSJ KPEKAV DFJAJC, YDR KV

GY IA XWJVJYBJ DYPA, FTR YDE ITBM IDWJ GY IA KFVJYBJ, EDWQ

DTR ADTW DEY VKPSKRGDY EGRM OJKW KYC RWJIFPGYZ.

XMGPGXXGKYV 2:12   *Clue: F = B*

81

LETTER TO THESSALONICA

ANQ INL SWTUYFV OAL NZH VOPSYH, OAL NZH FNHL MYUZU

GSHWUP, LWHYGP NZH QOJ ZAPN JNZ. OAL PSY FNHL TOEY JNZ

PN WAGHYOUY OAL OCNZAL WA FNRY NAY PNQOHL OANPSYH,

OAL PNQOHL OFF TYA, YRYA OU QY LN PNQOHL JNZ.

1 PSYUUOFNAWOAU 3:11–12   *Clue: S = H*

HAE EL LUSAWG OAP, XWLGSWLH, EFWH GSLD GSFG FWL PHWPVO,

BADRAWG GSL RLLXVLDTHKLK, JPYYAWG GSL ELFQ, XL YFGTLHG

GAEFWK FVV DLH. JLL GSFG HAHL WLHKLW LMTV RAW LMTV PHGA

FHO DFH; XPG LMLW RAVVAE GSFG ESTBS TJ NAAK, XAGS FDAHN

OAPWJLVMLJ, FHK GA FVV DLH.

1 GSLJJFVAHTFHJ 5:14–15   *Clue: Y = P*

FAMILIAR PHRASES

DLLI AL FW NJL FIIZL XM NJL LGL, JPBL AL KHBLQ NJL WJFBXT XM NJG TPHEW.

IWFZA 17:8

Clue: F = A

WLZ BHWULSRK DLHNN NOEW YQ WLR ATOUR; BOWL WLR ATOUR WTFRWLRP DLHNN WLRZ DOKF: ETP WLRZ DLHNN DRR RZR WT RZR, BLRK WLR NTPC DLHNN IPOKF HFHOK MOTK.

ODHOHL 52:8

Clue: T = O

CLR YN LB ALHA CYEE SEBHF CYAL OB? DRM QRC, YD Y LREF

OP ARQJVB, Y NLHEE JYZB VS ALB JLRNA.

XRU 13:19   *Clue: C = W*

GH GOW IWTL FWBTCW U TD IWTL, GOTG U CUXOG XTUA GOW

IWTL: U TC CTEW TSS GOUAXD GH TSS CWA, GOTG U CUXOG FP

TSS CWTAD DTJW DHCW.

1 BHVUAGOUTAD 9:22   *Clue: S = L*

YOU SWINE!

BGK LI RBYK QGPD PLIH, VD. BGK NLIG PLIC NIFI XDHI DQP, PLIC

NIGP YGPD PLI LIFK DE RNYGI: BGK, AILDMK, PLI NLDMI LIFK DE

RNYGI FBG WYDMIGPMC KDNG B RPIIZ ZMBXI YGPD PLI RIB, BGK

ZIFYRLIK YG PLI NBPIFR.

HBPPLIN 8:32   *Clue: F = R*

HV H FKYKB PT LPBC UO H VYUOK'V VOPDG, VP UV H THUE

YPWHO YAUIA UV YUGAPDG CUVIEKGUPO.

MEPZKERV 11:22   *Clue: Y = W*

JSZ EIK JUW UKGEKZ TS EIK GKRKSEI VYSEI, YS EIK GKRKSEKKSEI

ZJH YA EIK VYSEI, PNYS EIK VYPSEJTSG YA JUJUJE. JSZ EIK CJEKUG

ZKOUKJGKZ OYSETSPJQQH PSETQ EIK EKSEI VYSEI: TS EIK EKSEI VYSEI,

YS EIK ATUGE ZJH YA EIK VYSEI, CKUK EIK EYNG YA EIK VYPSEJTSG

GKKS.

XKSKGTG 8:4–5   *Clue: J =A*

QFRSNO RU AN FYY DGOFNY XPRU AUXPR WFOANY, FPB RSN

EOUESNRG UV TFFY VUXO SXPBONB FPB VDVRM, FPB RSN

EOUESNRG UV RSN QOUZNG VUXO SXPBONB, HSDWS NFR FR

INJNTNY'G RFTYN. GU FSFT GNPR XPRU FYY RSN WSDYBONP UV

DGOFNY, FPB QFRSNONB RSN EOUESNRG.

1 LDPQG 18:19–20   *Clue: Q = G*

BIBLE OCCUPATIONS

HPCW AMPQPKRQP AR XRZZU, UCW GUJJ MSAMPQ HSIRC, NMRHP

HLQCUIP SH ZPAPQ; MP SH JRWDPW SC AMP MRLHP RK RCP

HSIRC U AUCCPQ EB AMP HPU HSWP: NMR, NMPC MP GRIPAM,

HMUJJ HZPUV LCAR AMPP.

UGAH 10:32   *Clue: M = H*

YBMF KMTLT BMRCJ OH, BM TROHB LFHD HBMV, HBMI HBRH

RCM YBDEM BRXM FD FMMJ DG HBM UBITOSORF, QLH HBMI

HBRH RCM TOSW: O SRVM FDH HD SREE HBM COZBHMDLT, QLH

TOFFMCT HD CMUMFHRFSM.

VRCW 2:17   *Clue: C = R*

MORE BIBLE OCCUPATIONS

RSUY PYGBUJUL PODG, PYL GPWL RD POPKWPS, W BPG YD

TJDTSUR, YUWRSUJ BPG W P TJDTSUR'G GDY; CVR W BPG PY

SUJLOPY, PYL P XPRSUJUJ DN GZHDODJU NJVWR.

PODG 7:14

Clue: S = H

YWOWGDFXQ, H QFNKWDQOFGA, BAFMA OHYW QFNKWD

QADFZWQ LVD YFHZH, PDVXJAG ZV QOHNN JHFZ XZGV GAW

MDHLGQOWZ; BAVO AW MHNNWY GVJWGAWD BFGA GAW

BVDTOWZ VL NFTW VMMXCHGFVZ, HZY QHFY, QFDQ, EW TZVB

GAHG PE GAFQ MDHLG BW AHKW VXD BWHNGA.

HMGQ 19:24–25

Clue: M = C

EVEN MORE BIBLE OCCUPATIONS

VD MD XNKXPDZ, A MD KENVXSZPDS; KAJU, A MD LCSDZTDNNDTN,

HAT RKD JKDXR XSZ HAT RKD VXTUDM; VDOXEND RKD KXTLDNR

AH RKD HCDUZ CN FDTCNKDZ.

WADU 1:11

Clue: V = B

PUL ORQMQ QPGL MUJF JCR XRUJMTGFU, HF JCK SPK; PUL PQ

JCFM CPQJ NRZGRDRL, QF NR GJ LFUR MUJF JCRR. PUL CGQ

QRTDPUJ SPQ CRPZRL GU JCR QRZYQPER CFMT.

EPJJCRS 8:13

Clue: L = D

THEOLOGICAL TERMS

HXMAMOQAM JC PI HXM QOOMGWM QO QGM URNLVMGH

WJVM RBQG JEE VMG HQ WQGNMVGJHSQG; MTMG CQ PI HXM

ASLXHMQRCGMCC QO QGM HXM OAMM LSOH WJVM RBQG JEE

VMG RGHQ URCHSOSWJHSQG QO ESOM.

AQVJGC 5:18   *Clue: J = A*

OAORG MRRDEZLSU GD GJO KDEOCSDBAOZUO DK UDZ GJO

KMGJOE, GJEDWUJ PMSRGLKLRMGLDS DK GJO PVLELG, WSGD

DFOZLOSRO MSZ PVELSCALSU DK GJO FADDZ DK NOPWP RJELPG:

UEMRO WSGD XDW, MSZ VOMRO, FO HWAGLVALOZ.

1 VOGOE 1:2   *Clue: R = C*

STRONG WOMEN

HKLD MCLN KLGLA'I YTQL HFFO C DCTN FQ HKL HLDH, CDU

HFFO CD KCZZLA TD KLA KCDU, CDU YLDH IFQHNS PDHF KTZ,

CDU IZFHL HKL DCTN TDHF KTI HLZXNLI, CDU QCIHLDLU TH TDHF

HKL WAFPDU: QFA KL YCI QCIH CINLLX CDU YLCAS. IF KL UTLU.

MPUWLI 4:21   *Clue: I = S*

SOM MIQGNSW, S BNGBWIUILL, UWI XPYI GY CSBPMGUW, LWI

EAMZIM PLNSIC SU UWSU UPHI. SOM LWI MXICU AOMIN UWI

BSCH UNII GY MIQGNSW QIUXIIO NSHSW SOM QIUWIC PO HGAOU

IBWNSPH: SOM UWI RWPCMNIO GY PLNSIC RSHI AB UG WIN YGN

EAMZHIOU.

EAMZIL 4:4–5   *Clue: C = L*

NEHEMIAH'S STORY, PART 1

IGE F AIFE CGMK MRW QFGN, FB FM SXWIAW MRW QFGN, IGE

FB MRH AWLDIGM RIDW BKCGE BIDKCL FG MRH AFNRM, MRIM

MRKC YKCXEWAM AWGE PW CGMK ZCEIR, CGMK MRW JFMH KB

PH BIMRWLA' AWSCXJRLWA, MRIM F PIH OCFXE FM.

GWRWPFIR 2:5   *Clue: E = D*

X MXFI, A PCVCCKL ULCC, MCU HXE ULAHC CRF PC RUUCHUAGC

UX ULC ZFRNCF XB ULN VCFGRHU, RHI UX

ULC ZFRNCF XB ULN VCFGRHUV, ELX ICVAFC UX BCRF ULN HROC:

RHI ZFXVZCF, A ZFRN ULCC, ULN VCFGRHU ULAV IRN, RHI TFRHU

LAO OCFKN AH ULC VATLU XB ULAV ORH. BXF A ERV ULC DAHT'V

KQZPCRFCF.

HCLCOARL 1:11   *Clue: Z = P*

NEHEMIAH'S STORY, PART 2

IRLD VRKJR FNKMALA TG IRL VUMM, UGA IRLD IRUI FUBL

FNBALGY, VKIR IRTYL IRUI MUALA, LSLBD TGL VKIR TGL TW RKY

RUGAY VBTNQRI KG IRL VTBX, UGA VKIR IRL TIRLB RUGA RLMA U

VLUZTG.

GLRLCKUR 4:17   *Clue: F = B*

KD LPJ OBFF OBK ERCRKPJG. . . . BCG RL MBQJ LD IBKK, LPBL

OPJC BFF DXW JCJQRJK PJBWG LPJWJDE, BCG BFF LPJ PJBLPJC

LPBL OJWJ BYDXL XK KBO LPJKJ LPRCUK, LPJN OJWJ QXMP MBKL

GDOC RC LPJRW DOC JNJK: EDW LPJN IJWMJRHJG LPBL LPRK

ODWZ OBK OWDXUPL DE DXW UDG.

CJPJQRBP 6:15—16   *Clue: O = W*

REPENT!

DWCQ PYTP PGQK VKMOM FKRTH PC ZWKTNY, THU PC MTB,

WKZKHP: DCW PYK XGHRUCQ CD YKTIKH GM TP YTHU.

QTPPYKL 4:17 *Clue: Q = M*

PU Y OYHS, UPYRC RCS OBXM TBM, Y CPHS JB QOSPUFXS YJ RCS

MSPRC BD RCS AYILSM; KFR RCPR RCS AYILSM RFXJ DXBZ CYU

APV PJM OYHS.

SGSLYSO 33:11 *Clue: H = V*

NAMED ANGELS

EJF BNPDP OET OED SJ NPEXPJ: ASZNEPY EJF NST EJKPYT

LUHKNB EKESJTB BNP FDEKUJ; EJF BNP FDEKUJ LUHKNB EJF NST

EJKPYT.

DPXPYEBSUJ 12:7

Clue: F = D

YSM VTF YSAFU YSIZFGJSA IYJM PSVL TJD, J YD AYKGJFU, VTYV

IVYSM JS VTF OGFIFSEF LC ALM; YSM YD IFSV VL IOFYB PSVL

VTFF, YSM VL ITFZ VTFF VTFIF AUYM VJMJSAI.

UPBF 1:19

Clue: J = I

NOW HG FU SNH NU UVB DBZFOOFOZ GA UVBFP WSBCCFOZ
UVBPB, UVNU UVBQ ABNPBW OGU UVB CGPW: UVBPBAGPB UVB
CGPW HBOU CFGOH NIGOZ UVBI, SVFEV HCBS HGIB GA UVBI.

2 XFOZH 17:25

Clue: Z = G

WYZ QMSY RMS OGTOMSR RMWR FGTHUMR MAI FWDC KGTI RMS
QWX MSWGZ RMSGSTK, MS LWAZ, AR AL RMS IWY TK UTZ, QMT
QWL ZALTFSZASYR HYRT RMS QTGZ TK RMS NTGZ: RMSGSKTGS
RMS NTGZ MWRM ZSNAPSGSZ MAI HYRT RMS NATY, QMADM
MWRM RTGY MAI, WYZ LNWAY MAI.

1 CAYUL 13:26

Clue: N = L

SCRIPTURE ON SCRIPTURE

TJG VSP CJGK JT WJK BH UIBOX, YLK MJCPGTIR, YLK HSYGMPG

VSYL YLE VCJPKWPK HCJGK, MBPGOBLW PFPL VJ VSP KBFBKBLW

YHILKPG JT HJIR YLK HMBGBV, YLK JT VSP ZJBLVH YLK AYGGJC,

YLK BH Y KBHOPGLPG JT VSP VSJIWSVH YLK BLVPLVH JT VSP

SPYGV.

SPQGPCH 4:12

Clue: C = W

TSALGSI DFGB YGXBD, DFPD SA KXAKFQNC AY DFQ BNXGKDHXQ

GB AY PSC KXGJPDQ GSDQXKXQDPDGAS. YAX DFQ KXAKFQNC

NPZQ SAD GS AWM DGZQ RC DFQ LGWW AY ZPS: RHD FAWC ZQS

AY IAM BKPTQ PB DFQC LQXQ ZAJQM RC DFQ FAWC IFABD.

2 KQDQX 1:20–21

Clue: K = P

OFF TO SCHOOL

KQWLWTILW YQW APK KPE IHL EZQIIADPEYWL YI CLVFN HE

HFYI ZQLVEY, YQPY KW DVNQY CW UHEYVTVWB CS TPVYQ. CHY

PTYWL YQPY TPVYQ VE ZIDW, KW PLW FI AIFNWL HFBWL P

EZQIIADPEYWL.

NPAPYVPFE 3:24—25   *Clue: H = U*

CNR XIYJ TZOYFP XYFY IGFTYJYT, GJT CYMZYOYT JLR, CNR PQGSY

YOZM LD RIGR XGU CYDLFY RIY WNMRZRNTY, IY TYQGFRYT DFLW

RIYW, GJT PYQGFRYT RIY TZPEZQMYP, TZPQNRZJB TGZMU ZJ RIY

PEILLM LD LJY RUFGJJNP.

GERP 19:9   *Clue: M = L*

ELECT ME!

GPI UWC NWRFSICT QCRTM TPU KCU QPIT, TCRUWCI WXZRTM

SPTC XTK MPPS PI CZRF, UWXU UWC YJIYPLC PG MPS XNNPISRTM

UP CFCNURPT HRMWU LUXTS, TPU PG VPIAL, QJU PG WRH UWXU

NXFFCUW.

IPHXTL 9:11   *Clue: Q = B*

FRTCTMDCT BRT CXBRTC, ACTBRCTS, VWUT NWZWVTSIT BD QXET

ODLC IXZZWSV XSN TZTIBWDS GLCT: MDC WM OT ND BRTGT

BRWSVG, OT GRXZZ STUTC MXZZ: MDC GD XS TSBCXSIT GRXZZ AT

QWSWGBTCTN LSBD ODL XALSNXSBZO WSBD BRT TUTCZXGBWSV

EWSVNDQ DM DLC ZDCN XSN GXUWDLC YTGLG IRCWGB.

2 JTBTC 1:10–11   *Clue: U = V*

TOOLS IN THE BIBLE

GLT XL GSS FJSSP WFGW PFGSS ZU TJDDUT BJWF WFU

QGWWXOY, WFUVU PFGSS LXW OXQU WFJWFUV WFU IUGV XI

ZVJUVP GLT WFXVLP: ZCW JW PFGSS ZU IXV WFU PULTJLD IXVWF

XI XMUL, GLT IXV WFU WVUGTJLD XI SUPPUV OGWWSU.

JPGJGF 7:25   *Clue: D = G*

UQR PLY LKNJY, SLYQ MP SUJ MQ TNMBRMQH, SUJ TNMBP KZ

JPKQY CURY AYURE TYZKAY MP SUJ TAKNHLP PLMPLYA: JK PLUP

PLYAY SUJ QYMPLYA LUCCYA QKA UFY QKA UQE PKKB KZ MAKQ

LYUAR MP PLY LKNJY, SLMBY MP SUJ MQ TNMBRMQH.

1 OMQHJ 6:7   *Clue: N = U*

MTQ JOBT DBSBY JMU VGIB QGJT GLS GP SOB UORD, OB

JMEFBQ GT SOB JMSBY, SG HG SG ZBULU.

IMSSOBJ 14:29   *Clue: M = A*

GBDK MDGDF OREP, OECWDF RKP NHCP BRWD E KHKD; AQG

OQJB RO E BRWD NEWD E GBDD: EK GBD KRUD HL YDOQO

JBFEOG HL KRTRFDGB FEOD QM RKP SRCX.

RJGO 3:6   *Clue: H = O*

WS ZK XBDXOB, GPWHP FCB HFOOBN MK ZK AFZB, LPFOO

PRZMOB JPBZLBOYBL, FAN XCFK, FAN LBBT ZK SFHB, FAN JRCA

SCDZ JPBWC GWHTBN GFKL; JPBA GWOO W PBFC SCDZ PBFYBA,

FAN GWOO SDCQWYB JPBWC LWA, FAN GWOO PBFO JPBWC

OFAN.

2 HPCDAWHOBL 7:14   *Clue: C = R*

KWH FL JDL J ROENLG TLGLDJHVEG, J DEFJY ADVLNHOEEU, JG

OEYF GJHVEG, J ALRWYVJD ALEAYL.

1 ALHLD 2:9   *Clue: G = N*

SACRIFICES

PYI PRGPKPL NQQU NKB VQQI QH NKB RWGYN QHHBGOYA,

PYI ZPOI ON WFQY OEPPD KOE EQY; PYI KB NQQU NKB HOGB

OY KOE KPYI, PYI P UYOHB; PYI NKBS VBYN RQNK QH NKBL

NQABNKBG.

ABYBEOE 22:6   *Clue: R = B*

JL RUD AUVPU AVNN AD KWD OKYPRVHVDS RUWXMIU RUD

XHHDWVYI XH RUD JXSL XH TDOMO PUWVOR XYPD HXW KNN.

UDJWDAO 10:10   *Clue: O = S*

NOT MAN'S BEST FRIEND

FEL TY GPRPIPM FMKT KZFCP SBP MTXL, KFVNEO, SBP LTOK

KBFMM PFS GPRPIPM IV SBP DFMM TY GPRXPPM.

1 CNEOK 21:23   *Clue: L = D*

MNG ENUD FBKS YNWABDDSE WS: PFS BDDSWICV NM PFS ROYTSE

FBKS OXYCNDSE WS: PFSV AOSGYSE WV FBXED BXE WV MSSP.

ADBCW 22:16   *Clue: Y = C*

DWV MY PWJ LXJYYJI KFI VFXT GVPJFPKPJ, PWJ QMFO VZ QMFOY,

KFI XVHI VZ XVHIY; DWV VFXT WKPW MNNVHPKXMPT, IDJXXMFO

MF PWJ XMOWP DWMRW FV NKF RKF KGGHVKRW AFPV; DWVN

FV NKF WKPW YJJF, FVH RKF YJJ: PV DWVN LJ WVFVAH KFI

GVDJH JCJHXKYPMFO.

1 PMNVPWT 6:15–16   *Clue: G = P*

HNE AGJP PSMAG AGK GMBG SIV YNHAC NIK AGSA MIGSXMAKAG

KAKEIMAC, ZGNPK ISWK MP GNYC; M VZKYY MI AGK GMBG SIV

GNYC UYSRK, ZMAG GMW SYPN AGSA MP NH S RNIAEMAK SIV

GJWXYK PUMEMA.

MPSMSG 57:15   *Clue: H = F*

THE AWESOMENESS OF GOD, PART 2

GCBU ILST S, EAB SI RB! MAN S LR OUTAUB; DBYLOIB S LR L RLU

AM OUYPBLU PSFI, LUT S TEBPP SU GCB RSTIG AM L FBAFPB AM

OUYPBLU PSFI: MAN RSUB BVBI CLJB IBBU GCB QSUX, GCB PANT

AM CAIGI.

SILSLC 6:5

Clue: O = U

L HB HJDKH HEW RBTMH, YKT NTMLEELEM HEW YKT TEWLEM,

IHLYK YKT JRPW, XKLVK LI, HEW XKLVK XHI, HEW XKLVK LI YR

VRBT, YKT HJBLMKYG.

PTQTJHYLRE 1:8

Clue: I = S

SCENES BY THE RIVER

WZ CBFX SWPP UAC IFPWFEF NPJA CBFJF CSA JWLUJ, UFWCBFH

BFNHQFU GUCA CBX EAWTF, CBNC CBAG JBNPC CNQF AZ CBF

SNCFH AZ CBF HWEFH, NUM DAGH WC GDAU CBF MHX PNUM:

NUM CBF SNCFH SBWTB CBAG CNQFJC AGC AZ CBF HWEFH

JBNPP IFTARF IPAAM GDAU CBF MHX PNUM.

FOAMGJ 4:9   *Clue: G = U*

ZBQQT, OG DOBD IBV ITDO DOGG QGFAMH SAZHBM, DA IOAP

DOAC QBZGVD ITDMGVV, QGOAJH, DOG VBPG QBYDTXGDO, BMH

BJJ PGM EAPG DA OTP. SAOM BMVIGZGH BMH VBTH, B PBM

EBM ZGEGTWG MADOTML, GREGYD TD QG LTWGM OTP KZAP

OGBWGM.

SAOM 3:26–27   *Clue: S = J*

AN EVEN DOZEN

EKK HNRAR ECR HNR HPRKQR HCWVRA TM WACERK: ESU HNWA WA WH HNEH HNRWC MEHNRC AYEOR BSHT HNRD, ESU VKRAARU HNRD; RQRCJ TSR.

FRSRAWA 49:28

Clue: T = O

MXU HO AMQL OS CMII MGOLNEMNU, OYMO YL ELXO OYNSTJYSTO LKLND AHOD MXU KHZZMJL, CNLMAYHXJ MXU IYLEHXJ OYL JZMU OHUHXJI SG OYL PHXJUSQ SG JSU: MXU OYL OELZKL ELNL EHOY YHQ.

ZTPL 8:1

Clue: E = W

THE STORY OF ZACCHAEUS

MQE SF IVLJSA AV IFF BFILI YSV SF YMI; MQE RVLNE QVA PVU

ASF KUFII, ZFRMLIF SF YMI NWAANF VP IAMALUF. MQE SF UMQ

ZFPVUF, MQE RNWDZFE LK WQAV M IXRVDVUF AUFF AV IFF SWD:

PVU SF YMI AV KMII ASMA YMX.

NLCF 19:3–4

Clue: R = C

DTG RLKZK KDNG ZTEW QNC, EQNK GDU NK KDBYDENWT PWCL

EW EQNK QWZKL, VWJKWCZPQ DK QL DBKW NK D KWT WV

DSJDQDC. VWJ EQL KWT WV CDT NK PWCL EW KLLI DTG EW

KDYL EQDE XQNPQ XDK BWKE.

BZIL 19:9–10

Clue: N = I

MOSES' SISTER

LHF STO WGPBF FOZLNSOF ANPC PAA STO SLDONHLWGO; LHF,

DOTPGF, CENELC DOWLCO GOZNPBJ, ITESO LJ JHPI: LHF LLNPH

GPPQOF BZPH CENELC, LHF, DOTPGF, JTO ILJ GOZNPBJ.

HBCDONJ 12:10   *Clue: J = S*

PHN LCACPL MGY TAITGYMYKK, MGY KCKMYA IV PPAIH, MIIF

P MCLUAYZ CH GYA GPHN; PHN PZZ MGY DILYH DYHM IJM

PVMYA GYA DCMG MCLUAYZK PHN DCMG NPHOYK. PHN

LCACPL PHKDYAYN MGYL, KCHE SY MI MGY ZIAN, VIA GY GPMG

MACJLTGYN EZIACIJKZS.

YWINJK 15:20–21   *Clue: D = W*

COWS IN THE BIBLE

SLC PXC GSCT HOT ITSWH XY HOT TSMHO SYHTM OBW NBLC,

SLC ASHHZT SYHTM HOTBM NBLC, SLC TETMR HOBLP HOSH

AMTTVTHO FVXL HOT TSMHO SYHTM OBW NBLC: SLC PXC WSU

HOSH BH USW PXXC.

PTLTWBW 1:25   *Clue: P = G*

CBU MOP HESU ROCHH ICVP MOPP QHPBMPETR NB JEEUR,

NB MOP YSTNM EY MOG KEUG, CBU NB MOP YSTNM EY MOG

ZCMMHP, CBU NB MOP YSTNM EY MOG JSETBU, NB MOP HCBU

FONZO MOP HESU RFCSP TBME MOG YCMOPSR ME JNDP MOPP.

UPTMPSEBEIG 28:11   *Clue: H = L*

Y LYT, KMYE CZK KJZZVUQJ YEK YW KMR MYQR NQCIJF: KMJ LYT

YW VFZCJQ VF MJ KMCK LVPJKM FKZJGLKM CGT NYDJZ EGKY

MVF NJYNQJ. UQJFFJT UJ LYT.

NFCQX 68:35 *Clue: Q = L*

IVM DBPV LBP TFOM NID LBIL BP LHOVPM INCMP LF NPP, SFM

AITTPM HVLF BCU FHL FG LBP UCMNL FG LBP ZHNB, IVM NICM,

UFNPN, UFNPN. IVM BP NICM, BPOP IU C. IVM BP NICM, MOID

VFL VCSB BCLBPO: XHL FGG LBK NBFPN GOFU FGG LBK GPPL,

GFO LBP XTIAP DBPOPFV LBFH NLIVMPNL CN BFTK SOFHVM.

PYFMHN 3:4—5 *Clue: D = W*

MAKIN' MUSIC

MLBXPDEV FW QWNOMBGABM DE LMXGTM XEC IQTEM XEC

MLDODFNXG MWEVM, MDEVDEV XEC TXPDEV TBGWCQ DE QWNO

IBXOF FW FIB GWOC; VDADEV FIXEPM XGKXQM RWO XGG FIDEVM

NEFW VWC.

BLIBMDXEM 5:19–20

Clue: Q = Y

LG SJY SQAOHYSYQG LMV GCMEYQG NYQY LG WMY, SW OLPY WMY

GWAMV SW ZY JYLQV CM HQLCGCME LMV SJLMPCME SJY UWQV;

LMV NJYM SJYK UCBSYV AH SJYCQ RWCDY NCSJ SJY SQAOHYSG

LMV DKOZLUG LMV CMGSQAOYMSG WB OAGCDP, LMV HQLCGYV SJY

UWQV, GLKCME, BWQ JY CG EWWV; BWQ JCG OYQDK YMVAQYSJ

BWQ YRYQ: SJLS SJYM SJY JWAGY NLG BCUUYV NCSJ L DUWAV.

2 DJQWMCDUYG 5:13

Clue: O = M

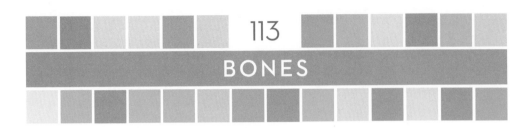
BONES

DRH LGWAW OGGP OIA TGRAW GX ZGWAUI EVOI IVL: XGN IA IDH

WONDVOMC WEGNR OIA SIVMHNAR GX VWNDAM, WDCVRY, YGH

EVMM WKNAMC BVWVO CGK; DRH CA WIDMM SDNNC KU LC

TGRAW DEDC IARSA EVOI CGK.

AFGHKW 13:19   *Clue: E = W*

QCUG LKSHU, LMM QCU RLMWLTQ PUT, LTO QSSE LALG QCU

FSOG SX HLBM, LTO QCU FSOWUH SX CWH HSTH, LTO FKSBVCQ

QCUP QS NLFUHC, LTO FBKWUO QCUWK FSTUH BTOUK QCU SLE

WT NLFUHC, LTO XLHQUO HURUT OLGH.

1 ZCKSTWZMUH 10:12   *Clue: F = B.*

FROM PSALM 119

AJLB KT DJMO BNRP J HPFDNVPH NDD LBP ZXHQKPELO IG LBT

KIXLB. J BNRP VPZIJFPH JE LBP ANT IG LBT LPOLJKIEJPO, NO

KXFB NO JE NDD VJFBPO. J AJDD KPHJLNLP JE LBT MVPFPMLO,

NEH BNRP VPOMPFL XELI LBT ANTO.

MONDK 119:13–15   *Clue: K = M*

VSWI CI PAYIEJNKAYSAV, KAY S JFKQQ ZIIH NFR QKO; RIK, S

JFKQQ ULJIEWI SN OSNF CR OFUQI FIKEN. CKZI CI NU VU SA NFI

HKNF UG NFR BUCCKAYCIANJ; GUE NFIEISA YU S YIQSVFN.

HJKQC 119:34–35   *Clue: Y = D*

MORE FROM PSALM 119

NCI IMJNC, A BAJR, GF WXBB AW NCH DIJPH: NIMPC DI NCH
FNMNXNIF. NCAX CMFN RIMBN LIBB LGNC NCH FIJTMSN, A BAJR,
MPPAJRGSY XSNA NCH LAJR. NIMPC DI YAAR KXRYDISN MSR
QSALBIRYI: WAJ G CMTI EIBGITIR NCH PADDMSRDISNF.

VFMBD 119:64–66

Clue: P = C

RMA PGUDAT MBYA EBGT B ZLBKA OIK CA: NAR G AKKAT LIR
OKIC RMN VKAUAVRZ. RMN RAZRGCILGAZ MBYA G RBDAL BZ
BL MAKGRBXA OIK AYAK: OIK RMAN BKA RMA KAQIGUGLX IO
CN MABKR. G MBYA GLUEGLAT CGLA MABKR RI VAKOIKC RMN
ZRBRSRAZ BEPBN, AYAL SLRI RMA ALT.

VZBEC 119:110–112

Clue: I = O

GIANT TROUBLE

SRE AGFZF MFRA UIA S LGSNKPUR UIA UY AGF LSNK UY AGF

KGPJPOAPRFO, RSNFE WUJPSAG, UY WSAG, MGUOF GFPWGA MSO

OPB LIQPAO SRE S OKSR.

1 OSNIFJ 17:4   *Clue: L = C*

KMH RFN KJKBM NDFPF CKV CKP KN JKND, CDFPF CKV K OKM

GA JPFKN VNKNEPF, CDGVF ABMJFPV KMH NGFV CFPF AGEP KMH

NCFMNR, VBW GM FKQD DKMH, KMH VBW GM FKQD AGGN KMH

DF KIVG CKV NDF VGM GA NDF JBKMN.

1 QDPGMBQIFV 20:6   *Clue: J = G*

KNL LBMK PMZYZ LOZ GNTK UK GMWBQMBMF NS PYHOMO UK

WBM HOEZ NS BMTNH WBM DUKI, GMBNQH, WBMTM ROFM LUZM

FMK STNF WBM MOZW WN PMTYZOQMF.

FOWWBML 2:1   *Clue: G = B*

HTS NPCIC HTCQPVWTF CHWS ITOL OAPK, VPTSPV OL ZHPCHV

OAP OAWTFC OAHO HVP ZHPCHV'C, HTS OL FLS OAP OAWTFC

OAHO HVP FLS'C.

KHVB 12:17   *Clue: F = G*

A BABYLONIAN KING

ROJS SJPTUOMISJWWMB ROJ FKSC LJSR RY CMROJB RYCJROJB
ROJ GBKSUJL, ROJ CYQJBSYBL, MSI ROJ UMGRMKSL, ROJ ETICJL,
ROJ RBJMLTBJBL, ROJ UYTSLJHHYBL, ROJ LOJBKZZL, MSI MHH ROJ
BTHJBL YZ ROJ GBYQKSUJL, RY UYVJ RY ROJ IJIKUMRKYS YZ ROJ
KVMCJ DOKUO SJPTUOMISJWWMB ROJ FKSC OMI LJR TG.

IMSKJH 3:2

Clue: I = D

SXTC CTYPRXFWCTBBFK GZFLT, FCW GFAW, YUTGGTW YT SXT
DQW QM GXFWKFRX, ITGXFRX, FCW FYTWCTDQ, VXQ XFSX GTCS
XAG FCDTU, FCW WTUAHTKTW XAG GTKHFCSG SXFS SKPGSTW AC
XAI, FCW XFHT RXFCDTW SXT LACD'G VQKW.

WFCATU 3:28

Clue: D = G

RULES FOR CHURCH LEADERS

J NGHFPT CFLE WKHC NL NZJWLZLHH, CFL FKHNJEV PX

PEL AGXL, IGYGZJEC, HPNLD, PX YPPV NLFJIGPKD, YGILE CP

FPHTGCJZGCR, JTC CP CLJOF; EPC YGILE CP AGEL, EP HCDGBLD,

EPC YDLLVR PX XGZCFR ZKODL; NKC TJCGLEC, EPC J NDJAZLD,

EPC OPILCPKH.

1 CGWPCFR 3:2—3   *Clue: D = R*

DTMR DTM DGMIJM ZBIIMQ DTM LXIDUDXQM KW DTM QUEZUSIME

XRDK DTML, BRQ EBUQ, UD UE RKD FMBEKR DTBD GM ETKXIQ

IMBJM DTM GKFQ KW AKQ, BRQ EMFJM DBPIME. GTMFMWKFM,

PFMDTFMR, IKKC OM KXD BLKRA OKX EMJMR LMR KW TKRMED

FMSKFD, WXII KW DTM TKIO ATKED BRQ GUEQKL.

BZDE 6:2—3   *Clue: Z = C*

SPIRITUAL U-TURNS

GEF SVNW NPYA, EG J CJMY, GEJNP NPY CWZO UWO, J PEMY

VW ICYEGSZY JV NPY OYENP WK NPY DJLRYO; XSN NPEN NPY

DJLRYO NSZV KZWA PJG DEF EVO CJMY: NSZV FY, NSZV FY

KZWA FWSZ YMJC DEFG; KWZ DPF DJCC FY OJY, W PWSGY WK

JGZEYC?

YBYRJYC 33:11

Clue: C = L

UXSQ, E PVIRMJWZWQA ITWJZSKQ, MVWUT UTK JESZ; NES W VH

HVSSWKZ XQUE BEX: VQZ W OWJJ UVRK BEX EQK EN V IWUB,

VQZ UOE EN V NVHWJB, VQZ W OWJJ PSWQA BEX UE GWEQ.

YKSKHWVT 3:14

Clue: E = O

HELLISH STUFF

YKO CG AUX UYKO NGGIKO AUII, PQA CA NGG: CA CJ RIAAIV GNV

AUII AN IKAIV CKAN TCGI SYCSIO, AUYK UYWCKD AZN UYKOJ AN

DN CKAN UITT, CKAN AUI GCVI AUYA KIWIV JUYTT RI MQIKPUIO:

ZUIVI AUICV ZNVS OCIAU KNA, YKO AUI GCVI CJ KNA MQIKPUIO.

SYVB 9:43–44

Clue: U = H

UML EQP NPUAE TUA EUFPM, UML TBEQ QBD EQP HUVAP

IZXIQPE EQUE TZXWRQE DBZUSVPA NPHXZP QBD, TBEQ TQBSQ

QP LPSPBCPL EQPD EQUE QUL ZPSPBCPL EQP DUZF XH EQP

NPUAE, UML EQPD EQUE TXZAQBIIPL QBA BDURP. EQPAP NXEQ

TPZP SUAE UVBCP BMEX U VUFP XH HBZP NWZMBMR TBEQ

NZBDAEXMP.

ZPCPVUEBXM 19:20

Clue: N = B

MORE HELLISH STUFF

GDA AMK TKCUTDB, CLJ DLGKBSKQSLV, CLJ AMK CGXNSLCGBK,

CLJ NDUJKUKUO, CLJ PMXUKNXLVKUO, CLJ OXUIKUKUO, CLJ

SJXBCAKUO, CLJ CBB BSCUO, OMCBB MCQK AMKSU WCUA SL

AMK BCEK PMSIM GDULKAM PSAM TSUK CLJ GUSNOAXLK: PMSIM

SO AMK OKIXLJ JKCAM.

UKQKBCASXL 21:8   *Clue: P = W*

GIBQ AMUMOWG, CDMC DI EMJ QPZ CDI CPZ VL DPG LPBRIO PB

YMCIO, MBQ NVVA EJ CVBRWI; LVO P ME CVOEIBCIQ PB CDPG

LAMEI. TWC MTOMDME GMPQ, GVB, OIEIETIO CDMC CDVW PB

CDJ APLICPEI OINIPFIQGC CDJ RVVQ CDPBRG, MBQ APHIYPGI

AMUMOWG IFPA CDPBRG: TWC BVY DI PG NVELVOCIQ, MBQ

CDVW MOC CVOEIBCIQ.

AWHI 16:24–25   *Clue: L = F*

HEAVENLY STUFF

ZSI AO PZTI LSQU NOPLP, EUJI, JORORXOJ RO HAOS QAUL
VUROPQ TSQU QAW DTSFIUR. ZSI NOPLP PZTI LSQU ATR, MOJTEW
T PZW LSQU QAOO, QUIZW PAZEQ QAUL XO HTQA RO TS
GZJZITPO.

ELDO 23:42–43

Clue: I = D

PWV O UWNQ ITGA P EPW, (QANJANH OW JAN YDVL, DH DTJ DS
JAN YDVL, O GPWWDJ JNMM: FDV UWDQNJA;) ADQ JAPJ AN QPI
GPTFAJ TK OWJD KPHPVOIN, PWV ANPHV TWIKNPUPYMN QDHVI,
QAOGA OJ OI WDJ MPQSTM SDH P EPW JD TJJNH.

2 GDHOWJAOPWI 12:3–4

Clue: T = U

MORE HEAVENLY STUFF

VPH GVTG DUZIMDHZGV JPFF P HTYZ T BPFFTI PX GVZ GZHBFZ DK

HS ODQ, TXQ VZ LVTFF OD XD HDIZ DCG: TXQ P JPFF JIPGZ CBDX

VPH GVZ XTHZ DK HS ODQ, TXQ GVZ XTHZ DK GVZ MPGS DK HS

ODQ, JVPMV PL XZJ AZICLTFZH, JVPMV MDHZGV QDJX DCG DK

VZTUZX KIDH HS ODQ: TXQ P JPFF JIPGZ CBDX VPH HS XZJ XTHZ.

IZUZFTGPDX 3:12   *Clue: F = L*

PWC CLKP GEE JLK AKWAEK CKVK XGAJSHKR, SJ NGDK JW

AGMM, JLGJ TKMZM GEMW XKSPI XGAJSHKR, GPR AVGFSPI, JLK

LKGBKP CGM WAKPKR, GPR JLK LWEF ILWMJ RKMNKPRKR SP G

XWRSEF MLGAK ESYK G RWBK ZAWP LSD, GPR G BWSNK NGDK

QVWD LKGBKP, CLSNL MGSR, JLWZ GVJ DF XKEWBKR MWP.

EZYK 3:21—22   *Clue: C = W*

LESSER-KNOWN DISCIPLES

GRENF FNCOI RDOT ICW, DTO CFUNHCTO, ATHE, ITM CF CO

OINO OITR MCAO WNDCLKFO OIXFKAL RDOT RF, NDE DTO RDOT

OIK MTHAE?

GTID 14:22   *Clue: F = S*

MS XWQS IULAP XOG, UI MXUG GUDSD OA YXS HWM, WAP YXS

JZUJXSYD, POP MZOYS, VSDLD UI AWKWZSYX, YXS DUA UI VUDSJX.

WAP AWYXWAWSH DWOP LAYU XOG, FWA YXSZS WAT NUUP

YXOAN FUGS ULY UI AWKWZSYX? JXOHOJ DWOYX LAYU XOG,

FUGS WAP DSS.

VUXA 1:45—46   *Clue: J = P*

BIBLICAL HORSES

SWA EXU XWARU WS MXOAOWX IUPE ZP IZEX XZR KXOAZWER

OPN IZEX XZR XWARUBUP ZPEW EXU RUO, OPN EXU GWAN

CAWYHXE OHOZP EXU IOEUAR WS EXU RUO YMWP EXUB; CYE EXU

KXZGNAUP WS ZRAOUG IUPE WP NAQ GOPN ZP EXU BZNRE WS

EXU RUO.

UVWNYR 15:19

Clue: N = D

KMY MXVZLN BPLL KM KNVR, UJHL BPL KNVR BPKB BPFX PKQB

UFQB, PFNQL CFN PFNQL, KMY TPKNJFB CFN TPKNJFB: KMY DL

DJUU CJOPB KOKJMQB BPLV JM BPL IUKJM, KMY QXNLUR DL

QPKUU ZL QBNFMOLN BPKM BPLR. KMY PL PLKNHLMLY XMBF

BPLJN AFJTL, KMY YJY QF.

1 HJMOQ 20:25

Clue: J = I

VILLAINS

IBVZIMPVG OLV NRQQVGAKHOL PHP KV KCNL VXHB: OLV BRGP

GVDIGP LHK INNRGPHMW OR LHA DRGSA: RE DLRK TV OLRC

DIGV IBAR; ERG LV LIOL WGVIOBU DHOLAORRP RCG DRGPA.

2 OHKROLU 4:14—15   *Clue: P = D*

NFM UW HUGBQUH ROGDF HG JNP UNFMR GF KGDMWONS

NJGFW; IGD HUWP UNM RUWAWM USK HUW LWGLJW GI

KGDMWONS: AUWDWIGDW UNKNF RGBQUH HG MWRHDGP NJJ

HUW YWAR HUNH AWDW HUDGBQUGBH HUW AUGJW TSFQMGK

GI NUNRBWDBR, WXWF HUW LWGLJW GI KGDMWONS.

WRHUWD 3:6   *Clue: R = S*

NOAH'S ARK

NTC EZQU QU EZB XNUZQPT JZQHZ EZPI UZNFE DNWB QE PX:

EZB FBTLEZ PX EZB NOW UZNFF RB EZOBB ZITCOBC HIRQEU,

EZB ROBNCEZ PX QE XQXEV HIRQEU, NTC EZB ZBQLZE PX QE

EZQOEV HIRQEU.

LBTBUQU 6:15

Clue: T = N

DVJFJ PJGD SG DPE BGX DPE RGDE GEBV SGDE DVJ BFH, DVJ LBYJ

BGX DVJ UJLBYJ, BC KEX VBX NELLBGXJX GEBV.

KJGJCSC 7:9

Clue: L = M

EXECUTIONS

VBI XCT, RTEBS RTWDNT EBXJNFLJTI DW CTN ODJCTN, XVEI, SEPT

OT CTNT UDCB RVYJEXJ'X CTVI EB V LCVNSTN.

OVJJCTZ 14:8

Clue: V = A

UY ALJB LHIXJZ LHEHI YI ALJ XHFFYPU ALHA LJ LHZ ODJOHDJZ

SYD EYDZJTHC. ALJI PHU ALJ QCIX'U PDHAL OHTCSCJZ.

JUALJD 7:10

Clue: H = A

FISH FRY

CLGTG FG TLZJJ GZC KX ZJJ CLZC ZMG PS CLG UZCGMT: ZJJ CLZC LZIG XPST ZSV TBZJGT TLZJJ FG GZC.

VGECGMKSYF 14:9

Clue: J = L

KM MGGI JLWI KM JLWF BWZW YGAW JG PKIX, JLWF MKB K CUZW GC YGKPM JLWZW, KIX CUML PKUX JLWZWGI, KIX TZWKX.

NGLI 21:9

Clue: W = E

PLANTING AND HARVESTING

FSCU SJRC VQNA NSCJF, LXF VSJWW GCJE FSQGAV: FSCU SJRC

EXF FSCTVCWRCV FQ EJOA, LXF VSJWW AQF EGQHOF: JAY FSCU

VSJWW LC JVSJTCY QH UQXG GCRCAXCV LCDJXVC QH FSC

HOCGDC JAKCG QH FSC WQGY.

BCGCTOJS 12:13

Clue: T = M

QD FAC ODJDMTDO; VAO MP FAC SAJIDO: RAE BNKCPADTDE K

SKF PABDCN, CNKC PNKYY ND KYPA EDKG. RAE ND CNKC PABDCN

CA NMP RYDPN PNKYY AR CND RYDPN EDKG JAEEXGCMAF; QXC

ND CNKC PABDCN CA CND PGMEMC PNKYY AR CND PGMEMC

EDKG YMRD DTDEYKPCMFV.

VKYKCMKFP 6:7–8

Clue: P = S

OTHER FARM ANALOGIES

QYKOB AUE SO SE YSO YUEJ, UEJ YB QSZZ FYTKGXYZL WGTXB

YSO AZKKT, UEJ XUFYBT YSO QYBUF SEFK FYB XUTEBT; DGF YB

QSZZ DGTE GW FYB MYUAA QSFY GEIGBEMYUDZB ASTB.

RUFFYBQ 3:12   *Clue: Q = W*

MYI OC BZ IGC DBJFWC, LPS IGC GNSUCDI BD SBMC: JPVC, RCI

OPY QPEZ; LPS IGC MSCDD BD LYWW, IGC LNID PUCSLWPE; LPS

IGCBS EBJFCQZCDD BD RSCNI.

TPCW 3:13   *Clue: S = R*

ATHLETICS IN THE BIBLE

B IQVTVSFTV JF TDR, RFI YJ DRKVTIYBRWH; JF SBXQI B, RFI YJ

FRV IQYI MVYIVIQ IQV YBT: MDI B CVVU DREVT GH MFEH, YRE

MTBRX BI BRIF JDMLVKIBFR: WVJI IQYI MH YRH GVYRJ, NQVR B

QYOV UTVYKQVE IF FIQVTJ, B GHJVWS JQFDWE MV Y KYJIYNYH.

1 KFTBRIQBYRJ 9:26–27   *Clue: T = R*

AKRSRGLSR VRRUYJ AR IZVL ISR XLFCIVVRE IMLTO AUOK VL JSRIO

I XZLTE LG AUOYRVVRV, ZRO TV ZIB IVUER RNRSB ARUJKO, IYE

OKR VUY AKUXK ELOK VL RIVUZB MRVRO TV, IYE ZRO TV STY

AUOK CIOURYXR OKR SIXR OKIO UV VRO MRGLSR TV.

KRMSRAV 12:1   *Clue: X = C*

WEAPONRY

UZA KXC PDMA YUOA EZKD BDYXEU, YKMCKWX DEK KXC YICUM

KXUK OY OZ KXH XUZA KDNUMA UO; GDM O NOPP JOFC OK

OZKD KXOZC XUZA. UZA BDYXEU YKMCKWXCA DEK KXC YICUM

KXUK XC XUA OZ XOY XUZA KDNUMA KXC WOKH.

BDYXEU 8:18

Clue: U = A

HDURT BOOUHR BOT RDBOZ, BJI BXX GDTLO SUHR STJG, GDTLO

DUORTR' DUUYR RDBXX ST FUPJGTI XLCT YXLJG, BJI GDTLO

HDTTXR XLCT B HDLOXHLJI.

LRBLBD 5:28

Clue: H = W

HOW BIG IS GOD?

WF P W MXZ WS KWRZ, NWPSK SKV EXJZ, WRZ RXS W MXZ

WTWJ XTT? IWR WRO KPZV KPFNVET PR NVIJVS QEWIVN SKWS P

NKWEE RXS NVV KPF? NWPSK SKV EXJZ. ZX RXS P TPEE KVWBVR

WRZ VWJSK? NWPSK SKV EXJZ.

YVJVFPWK 23:23—24

Clue: K = H

NKHCKPD LKSUU H XW BDWE CKF LOHDHC? WD NKHCKPD LKSUU

H BUPP BDWE CKF ODPLPVTP? HB H SLTPVI MO HVCW KPSRPV,

CKWM SDC CKPDP: HB H ESJP EF QPI HV KPUU, QPKWUI, CKWM

SDC CKPDP.

OLSUE 139:7—8

Clue: L = S

BIBLICAL KISSES

XPUTN EJW IUMIK EUP XPI IDAPIKPU; UHAKIPDMQJPQQ EJW

BPETP KESP OHQQPW PETK DIKPU.

BQEZX 85:10

Clue: E = A

EIXU WBVQM LBE OBVIXC HIX TBDPIHXO QR CBMBU IKL AQHIXO'L

MOQHIXO, BUT HIX LIXXS QR CBMBU IKL AQHIXO'L MOQHIXO,

HIBH WBVQM EXUH UXBO, BUT OQCCXT HIX LHQUX ROQA

HIX EXCC'L AQDHI, BUT EBHXOXT HIX RCQVG QR CBMBU IKL

AQHIXO'L MOQHIXO. BUT WBVQM GKLLXT OBVIXC.

PXUXLKL 29:10—11

Clue: M = B

HONESTY IS THE BEST POLICY

J SJWCR IJWJBFR OC JITHOBJGOTB GT GAR WTUY: IQG J NQCG

XROVAG OC AOC YRWOVAG.

LUTMRUIC 11:1   *Clue: R = E*

PVR DEPD TO GFD ZV DEO VOI UPV, IEYME PQDOW LZR

YA MWOPDOR YV WYLEDOZFAVOAA PVR DWFO EZXYVOAA.

IEOWOQZWO GFDDYVL PIPT XTYVL, AGOPJ OSOWT UPV DWFDE

IYDE EYA VOYLEKZFW: QZW IO PWO UOUKOWA ZVO ZQ

PVZDEOW.

OGEOAYPVA 4:24—25   *Clue: G = P*

VPI DSB KUNI IBKEZBNBI ED VKTU, VPI DSB REPF DSBNBUA, EPDU DSB

SVPI UA ETNVBK; VPI SB TYUDB ED GEDS DSB BIFB UA DSB TGUNI,

VPI VKK DSB TUOKT DSVD GBNB DSBNBEP; SB KBD PUPB NBYVEP EP

ED; XOD IEI OPDU DSB REPF DSBNBUA VT SB IEI OPDU DSB REPF UA

LBNEWSU.

LUTSOV 10:30

Clue: K = L

NBD EHYKZ RFAD FYX WLJKBN, NBDY WLJKBN NBD EHYKZ LW

RFYFFY HY NFFYFRB SG NBD QFNDUZ LW ADKHXXL; NBDG NLLO

YL KFHY LW ALYDG. NBDG WLJKBN WULA BDFMDY; NBD ZNFUZ

HY NBDHU RLJUZDZ WLJKBN FKFHYZN ZHZDUF.

IJXKDZ 5:19–20

Clue: Y = N

UPC LI RUOC TPVN LOA, O UA VLI KNGC VLUV HGNTBLV VLII

NTV NY TG NY VLI ZLUKCIIR, VN BOMI VLII VLOR KUPC VN

OPLIGOV OV.

BIPIROR 15:7 *Clue: C = D*

XAPEP CMF M SMI YI XAP WMIU DV LK, CADFP IMSP CMF GDO;

MIU XAMX SMI CMF BPEVPZX MIU LBEYHAX, MIU DIP XAMX

VPMEPU HDU, MIU PFZAPCPU PQYW.

GDO 1:1 *Clue: D = O*

NBG GNKLG CNLG TQ RPWXW DJHGX LB PLX PWNHR, NBG DNX

XJHW NSHNLG JS NVPLXP RPW MLBI JS INRP. NBG PW VPNBIWG PLX

ZWPNKLJTH ZWSJHW RPWO, NBG SWLIBWG PLOXWCS ONG LB RPWLH

PNBGX, NBG XVHNZZCWG JB RPW GJJHX JS RPW INRW, NBG

CWR PLX XQLRRCW SNCC GJDB TQJB PLX ZWNHG.

1 XNOTWC 21:12–13

Clue: I = G

WUJPQJ JMVO LVPN M AGQO KGVHU, SMQA, PNGQ MBP IUJVOU

PNTJUAW; XQHN AUMBZVZD OGPN XMFU PNUU XMO. IQP NU

JMVO, V MX ZGP XMO, XGJP ZGIAU WUJPQJ; IQP JSUMF WGBPN

PNU LGBOJ GW PBQPN MZO JGIUBZUJJ.

MHPJ 26:24–25

Clue: M = A

UYZ YED, BOFFBH WJOBZCHY, UAOZH OY JOT; FJUF, DJHY

JH RJUBB UIIHUC, DH TUK JUSH WEYMOZHYWH, UYZ YEF AH

URJUTHZ AHMECH JOT UF JOR WETOYQ.

1 LEJY 2:28

Clue: Y = N

FTAD BAOA FTAOA ROIQLTF QDFI TGV PGFFPA JTGPUOAD,

FTSF TA NTIQPU HQF TGN TSDUN ID FTAV, SDU HOSX: SDU FTA

UGNJGHPAN OARQWAU FTAV. RQF YANQN NSGU, NQZZAO PGFFPA

JTGPUOAD, SDU ZIORGU FTAV DIF, FI JIVA QDFI VA: ZIO IZ NQJT

GN FTA WGDLUIV IZ TASMAD.

VSFFTAB 19:13—14

Clue: Z = F

IT'S MAGIC

OKWVW NKTQQ PGO XW AGZPU TCGPM RGZ TPR GPW OKTO

CTLWOK KSN NGP GV KSN UTZMKOWV OG FTNN OKVGZMK OKW

ASVW, GV OKTO ZNWOK USDSPTOSGP, GV TP GXNWVDWV GA

OSCWN, GV TP WPEKTPOWV, GV T JSOEK.

UWZOWVGPGCR 18:10   *Clue: K = H*

I NIZ IMUS SC XSNIZ OTIO TIOT I VINJMJIC UGJCJO, SC OTIO JU

I XJDICQ, UTIMM URCPMK FP GRO OS QPIOT: OTPK UTIMM UOSZP

OTPN XJOT UOSZPU: OTPJC FMSSQ UTIMM FP RGSZ OTPN.

MPAJOJHRU 20:27   *Clue: X = W*

CRAFTSMANSHIP

VPSBAM TA HFA OCG HFCH OCZAHF CGQ NSCJAG DS ODIHAG

KOCNA, CG CTDOKGCHKDG PGHD HFA IDSM, HFA XDSZ DY HFA

FCGMB DY HFA VSCYHBOCG, CGM EPHHAHF KH KG C BAVSAH

EICVA. CGM CII HFA EADEIA BFCII CGBXAS CGM BCQ, COAG.

MAPHASDGDOQ 27:15   *Clue: P = U*

EDH NUL KFCTL FY UEGJLGB, EDH AVBCTCEDB, EDH FY JCJLGB,

EDH NGVAJLNLGB, BUEZZ XL ULEGH DF AFGL EN EZZ CD NULL;

EDH DF TGEYNBAED, FY OUENBFLKLG TGEYN UL XL, BUEZZ XL

YFVDH EDR AFGL CD NULL; EDH NUL BFVDH FY E ACZZBNFDL

BUEZZ XL ULEGH DF AFGL EN EZZ CD NULL.

GLKLZENCFD 18:22   *Clue: X = B*

GOD'S LOVE

MUN YSKP YK YKNK HKJ YEJSUQJ AJNKPFJS, EP GQK JELK

BSNEAJ GEKG MUN JSK QPFUGDH.

NULTPA 5:6   *Clue: Y = W*

RUE A IV MBEZYITBT, QJIQ DBAQJBE TBIQJ, DUE SARB, DUE

IDLBSZ, DUE MEADGAMISAQABZ, DUE MUFBEZ, DUE QJADLZ

MEBZBDQ, DUE QJADLZ QU GUVB, DUE JBALJQ, DUE TBMQJ, DUE

IDH UQJBE GEBIQYEB, ZJISS OB IOSB QU ZBMIEIQB YZ REUV QJB

SUXB UR LUT, FJAGJ AZ AD GJEAZQ NBZYZ UYE SUET.

EUVIDZ 8:38–39   *Clue: M = P*

145

ON THE VINE

WNCKQ CM SQ, WMK C CM IHY. WB EAQ NUWMFA FWMMHE

NQWU VUYCE HV CEBQZV, QJFQLE CE WNCKQ CM EAQ DCMQ;

MH SHUQ FWM IQ, QJFQLE IQ WNCKQ CM SQ.

RHAM 15:4   *Clue: W = A*

LPK QFR LKMBQ PL QFR AIBKBQ BA BO ECC SPPYORAA EOY

KBSFQRPMAORAA EOY QKMQF; IKPJBOS XFEQ BA EDDRIQETCR

MOQP QFR CPKY.

RIFRABEOA 5:9—10   *Clue: Q = T*

JESUS DESCRIBES HIMSELF

HSML WXYUM GMWIW YJYOL ILHE HSMR, WYCOLJ, O YR HSM

VOJSH ED HSM BEKVN: SM HSYH DEVVEBMHS RM WSYVV LEH

BYVU OL NYKULMWW, ZIH WSYVV SYPM HSM VOJSH ED VODM.

GESL 8:12   *Clue: V = L*

B DO IVS TUUQ: JP OS BC DGP ODG SGISQ BG, VS HVDKK JS

HDAST, DGT HVDKK YU BG DGT UXI, DGT CBGT WDHIXQS. IVS

IVBSC ZUOSIV GUI, JXI CUQ IU HISDK, DGT IU RBKK, DGT IU

TSHIQUP: B DO ZUOS IVDI IVSP OBYVI VDAS KBCS, DGT IVDI IVSP

OBYVI VDAS BI OUQS DJXGTDGIKP.

NUVG 10:9–10   *Clue: B = I*

PAUL DESCRIBES HIMSELF

XN SJUNH LMP UC PXN SLMCSUO, WNC TCH RJNPXJNC, U

TW T KXTJUINN, PXN ILC LD T KXTJUINN: LD PXN XLKN TCH

JNIMJJNSPULC LD PXN HNTH U TW STOONH UC AMNIPULC.

TSPI 23:6   *Clue: K = P*

RGSRNHRGYKX PVK KGFVPV XJT, ID PVK YPIRA ID GYSJKE, ID PVK

PSGZK ID ZKCUJHGC, JC VKZSKL ID PVK VKZSKLY; JY PINRVGCF

PVK EJL, J QVJSGYKK; RICRKSCGCF MKJE, QKSYKRNPGCF PVK

RVNSRV; PINRVGCF PVK SGFVPKINYCKYY LVGRV GY GC PVK EJL,

ZEJHKEKYY.

QVGEGQQGJCY 3:5—6   *Clue: P = T*

I'M DEPRESSED

BJK RL NBYH LC IBOO, GDHJ LDH OTJ KRK BZROH, LDBL SCK

IZHIBZHK B MHDHYHJL HBOL GRJK; BJK LDH OTJ PHBL TICJ LDH

DHBK CA FCJBD, LDBL DH ABRJLHK, BJK GRODHK RJ DRYOHUA LC

KRH, BJK OBRK, RL RO PHLLHZ ACZ YH LC KRH LDBJ LC URMH.

FCJBD   4:8   *Clue: O = S*

QZV AB AUIPBJE KBSV H YHT'P RNZCSBT USVN VAB KUJYBCSBPP,

HSY WHIB HSY PHV YNKS ZSYBC H RZSUMBC VCBB: HSY AB

CBOZBPVBY ENC AUIPBJE VAHV AB IUFAV YUB; HSY PHUY, UV

UP BSNZFA; SNK, N JNCY, VHXB HKHT IT JUEB; ENC U HI SNV

QBVVBC VAHS IT EHVABCP.

1 XUSFP 19:4   *Clue: A = H*

I'M FULL OF JOY

O ZOBB CBGPP XAG BEYI DX DBB XOWGP: AOP RYDOPG PADBB

SELXOLKDBBV CG OL WV WEKXA. WV PEKB PADBB WDNG AGY

CEDPX OL XAG BEYI: XAG AKWCBG PADBB AGDY XAGYGEM, DLI

CG FBDI.

RPDBW 34:1–2   *Clue: W = M*

GOA FGLJ RGTA, FJ RHNB AHIU FGSOTEJ IUW BHLA, GOA FJ

RMTLTI UGIU LWXHTQWA TO SHA FJ RGYTHNL. EHL UW UGIU

LWSGLAWA IUW BHD WRIGIW HE UTR UGOAFGTAWO: EHL,

PWUHBA, ELHF UWOQWEHLIU GBB SWOWLGITHOR RUGBB QGBB

FW PBWRRWA.

BNCW 1:46–48   *Clue: A = D*

SOLAR OCCURRENCES

USG REB FQS FRCCG FRZNN, USG REB HCCS FRUKBG, QSRZN

REB ABCANB EUG UJBSOBG REBHFBNJBF QACS REBZD BSBHZBF.

ZF SCR REZF MDZRRBS ZS REB XCCT CY PUFEBD? FC REB FQS

FRCCG FRZNN ZS REB HZGFR CY EBUJBS.

PCFEQU 10:13

Clue: S = N

KIL GM OKQ KVTDM MNJ QGZMN NTDH, KIL MNJHJ OKQ K

LKHFIJQQ TSJH KXX MNJ JKHMN DIMGX MNJ IGIMN NTDH. KIL

MNJ QDI OKQ LKHFIJL, KIL MNJ SJGX TW MNJ MJBYXJ OKQ

HJIM GI MNJ BGLQM. KIL ONJI PJQDQ NKL EHGJL OGMN K

XTDL STGEJ, NJ QKGL, WKMNJH, GIMT MNC NKILQ G ETBBJIL BC

QYGHGM.

XDFJ 23:44—46

Clue: L = D

LET'S PARTY

CAW PGSA HGSES WCTE PSQS SYVJQSW, HGS NJAR LCWS

C OSCEH FAHD CKK HGS VSDVKS HGCH PSQS VQSESAH JA

EGFEGCA HGS VCKCZS, XDHG FAHD RQSCH CAW ELCKK, ESUSA

WCTE, JA HGS ZDFQH DO HGS RCQWSA DO HGS NJAR'E VCKCZS.

SEHGSQ 1:5

Clue: R = G

TSYC HSXE IMUYDH M BOCCYL XL M DEFFYL, PMVV CXH HSG

JLOYCBD, CXL HSG RLYHSLYC, CYOHSYL HSG UOCDIYC, CXL HSG

LOPS CYOQSRXELD; VYDH HSYG MVDX ROB HSYY MQMOC, MCB

M LYPXIFYCPY RY IMBY HSYY. REH TSYC HSXE IMUYDH M JYMDH,

PMVV HSY FXXL, HSY IMOIYB, HSY VMIY, HSY RVOCB: MCB HSXE

DSMVH RY RVYDDYB.

VEUY 14:12–14

Clue: V = L

PROTECTED

EPR UMQPE MW OCY WLRUE, EPR BCN MW CE PCUB: KRE IW

EPRYROZYR DCWE ZOO EPR GZYVW ZO BCYVURWW, CUB KRE IW

LIE ZU EPR CYXZIY ZO KMQPE.

YZXCUW 13:12   *Clue: Y = R*

LZC UM COA YOUPA SDVUZD UN EUI, COSC HA VSH GA SGPA

CU BCSMI SESKMBC COA YKPAB UN COA IARKP. NUD YA

YDABCPA MUC SESKMBC NPABO SMI GPUUI, GZC SESKMBC

LDKMXKLSPKCKAB, SESKMBC LUYADB, SESKMBC COA DZPADB

UN COA ISDQMABB UN COKB YUDPI, SESKMBC BLKDKCZSP

YKXQAIMABB KM OKEO LPSXAB.

ALOABKSMB 6:11–12   *Clue: L = P*

QO VUSZB UQLUBUG, DBFP BF DUT XUAAFY ZJ MJ JRZ SPZJ U

CAUXF DBSXB BF TBJRAY UVZFL LFXFSWF VJL UP SPBFLSZUPXF,

JQFOFY; UPY BF DFPZ JRZ, PJZ IPJDSPM DBSZBFL BF DFPZ.

BFQLFDT 11:8   *Clue: S = I*

AWOI VOIA YPIX EQUPE PI, QIE LQA COJDFO AWO BDFE, QIE WO

LQPE, VWD QR P, D BDFE XDE? QIE VWQA PL RG WDNLO, AWQA

AWDN WQLA CFDNXWA RO WPAWOFAD?

2 LQRNOB 7:18   *Clue: E = D*

MORE FAMOUS NAMES

EWG ITWV OYHYPYW OCEHH FS FHSOOSG, EWG JCS JCZYWS YU

GENTG OCEHH FS SOJEFHTOCSG FSUYZS JCS HYZG UYZ SNSZ.

1 ITWVO 2:45   *Clue: H = L*

YESL IWLKYEKL KLC CKHNC VKCS K PWHSLKLY, JSPKFTS ES

BWHSC ENV KT ENT WRL TWFB.

1 TKVFSB 18:3   *Clue: E = H*

THE TEMPTATION OF CHRIST

JUK ERHAH SRXUL OANN GO DVR VGNT LVGHD IRDAIURK OIGB

EGIKJU, JUK QJH NRK ST DVR HMXIXD XUDG DVR QXNKRIURHH,

SRXUL OGIDT KJTH DRBMDRK GO DVR KRYXN. JUK XU DVGHR

KJTH VR KXK RJD UGDVXUL.

NACR 4:1–2

Clue: Q = W

WOO RETD XAYLU YTOO T BTKL RELL, WMH REL BOAUQ AV

RELF: VAU REWR TD HLOTKLULH IMRA FL; WMH RA YEAFDALKLU

T YTOO T BTKL TR. TV REAI RELULVAUL YTOR YAUDETX FL, WOO

DEWOO NL RETML. WMH CLDID WMDYLULH WMH DWTH IMRA

ETF, BLR RELL NLETMH FL, DWRWM: VAU TR TD YUTRRLM, REAI

DEWOR YAUDETX REL OAUH REQ BAH.

OIPL 4:6–8

Clue: H = D

JS HR ORZSWCRJI XRWCRTWPR TWK GRPSHLRWPR; JIRQG MSSJ YITZZ YZQKR QW KFR JQHR: MSG JIR KTN SM JIRQG PTZTHQJN QY TJ ITWK, TWK JIR JIQWCY JITJ YITZZ PSHR FLSW JIRH HTAR ITYJR.

KRFJRGSWSHN 32:35

Clue: T = A

DYP VU VEOJ VEYV YTO UH Y HOYTHFN EOYTV, GO DVTUIL, HOYT IUV: GOEUNB, PUFT LUB ZANN XUJO ZAVE MOILOYIXO, OMOI LUB ZAVE Y TOXUJQOIXO; EO ZANN XUJO YIB DYMO PUF.

ADYAYE 35:4

Clue: A = I

VALUABLES

TFM CRV FW DLQ VLFQBHCYHB MQHRBFQHB US GHRYHS, NGHQH

SHUMGHQ ZLMG SLQ QFBM KLMG JLQQFWM, RSK NGHQH

MGUHYHB KL SLM TQHRP MGQLFOG SLQ BMHRC: DLQ NGHQH

VLFQ MQHRBFQH UB, MGHQH NUCC VLFQ GHRQM TH RCBL.

ZRMMGHN 6:20—21   *Clue: C = L*

AEI FVH MPNH ETIV UNR, IUVE ZVVD, IUNM TNFUI IUC MVED

MUPDD AG SGKENSGH VZ IUGG: IUGT YUVMG MUPDD IUVMG

IUNTFM AG, YUNQU IUVE UPMI BSVXNHGH? MV NM UG IUPI

DPCGIU EB ISGPMESG ZVS UNRMGDZ, PTH NM TVI SNQU IVYPSH

FVH.

DELG 12:20—21   *Clue: S = R*

GJL NSPT RPOP GEE GQGXPL, ZJWAQBYS NSGN NSPT KBPWNZAJPL

GQAJD NSPQWPEMPW, WGTZJD, RSGN NSZJD ZW NSZW? RSGN

JPR LAYNOZJP ZW NSZW? UAO RZNS GBNSAOZNT YAQQGJLPNS SP

PMPJ NSP BJYEPGJ WFZOZNW, GJL NSPT LA ACPT SZQ.

QGOI 1:27   *Clue: G = A*

NTA JKHNDNKPA XGJA NRUANTAV, GEP LAVA XRECRKEPAP,

SAXGKYA NTGN AQAVM JGE TAGVP NTAJ YZAGO DE TDY RLE

HGEUKGUA. GEP NTAM LAVA GHH GJGBAP GEP JGVQAHHAP,

YGMDEU REA NR GERNTAV, SATRHP, GVA ERN GHH NTAYA LTDXT

YZAGO UGHDHGAGEY? GEP TRL TAGV LA AQAVM JGE DE RKV RLE

NREUKA?

GXNY 2:6—8   *Clue: P = D*

THE SHEPHERD

GNV EFSP FS TDE VFS CNYVUVNLST, FS EDT CAKSL EUVF

BACHDTTUAP AP VFSC, GSBDNTS VFSJ MDUPVSL, DPL ESZS

TBDVVSZSL DGZADL, DT TFSSH FDKUPO PA TFSHFSZL.

CDVVFSE 9:36   *Clue: A = O*

H TN ABG XLLK WBGEBGUK, TSK CSLF NR WBGGE, TSK TN CSLFS

LP NHSG. TW ABG PTABGU CSLFGAB NG, GQGS WL CSLF H ABG

PTABGU: TSK H ZTR KLFS NR ZHPG PLU ABG WBGGE.

YLBS 10:14—15   *Clue: N = M*

FRUIT OF THE VINE

MI YIC MDLYO KLYP YID BCDIYE MDLYO, CUIX, YID CUW

BIYB KLCU CUPP, KUPY WP EI LYCI CUP CGHPDYGTFP IS CUP

TIYEDPEGCLIY, FPBC WP MLP: LC BUGFF HP G BCGCXCP SID PJPD

CUDIXEUIXC WIXD EPYPDGCLIYB.

FPJLCLTXB 10:9
Clue: E = G

EWRMJEW, T XEPL LJY, MJ MIWD, WSWU MITR BPL, MIWTE KPUBR,

MIWTE STUWLPEBR, MIWTE JKTSWLPEBR, PUB MIWTE IJYRWR,

PKRJ MIW IYUBEWBMI XPEM JV MIW DJUWL, PUB JV MIW ZJEU,

MIW QTUW, PUB MIW JTK, MIPM LW WGPZM JV MIWD.

UWIWDTPI 5:11
Clue: R = S

LOVE SONGS

NU MLD NSSOD MJDD NECPT MLD MJDDU CG MLD VCCA, UC

KU EX QDOCYDA NECPT MLD UCPU. K UNM ACVP WPADJ LKU

ULNACV VKML TJDNM ADOKTLM, NPA LKU GJWKM VNU UVDDM

MC EX MNUMD.

UCPT CG UCOCECP 2:3   *Clue: V = W*

FXY KCQO QP JFB HXLT, UB PQPJTO, UB PMXZPT! FXY UZGF

STJJTO QP JFB HXLT JFCA YQAT! CAW JFT PUTHH XK JFQAT

XQAJUTAJP JFCA CHH PMQGTP!

PXAR XK PXHXUXA 4:10   *Clue: J = T*

NYR MPGLG, ONHJAYD KB UIP GPN SC DNHAHPP, GNO UOS

KQPUIQPY, GAXSY FNHHPR WPUPQ, NYR NYRQPO IAG KQSUIPQ,

FNGUAYD N YPU AYUS UIP GPN: CSQ UIPB OPQP CAGIPQG.

XNUUIPO 4:18   *Clue: A = I*

DAB DI LRC KRCQRSFBC, TAKUBH, CRYDA SBVBU'C JUDVLBU,

CTRVL MAVD LRY, VLBUB RC T FTK LBUB, HLRQL LTVL IROB

JTUFBG FDTOBC, TAK VHD CYTFF IRCLBC: JMV HLTV TUB VLBG

TYDAP CD YTAG?

XDLA 6:8—9   *Clue: D = O*

MYSTERIES

FRJMJ VJ FRMJJ FRDAQZ TRDLR IMJ FEE TEAHJMSXG SEM PJ,

WJI, SEXM TRDLR D UAET AEF: FRJ TIW ES IA JIQGJ DA FRJ IDM;

FRJ TIW ES I ZJMCJAF XCEA I MELU; FRJ TIW ES I ZRDC DA FRJ

PDHZF ES FRJ ZJI; IAH FRJ TIW ES I PIA TDFR I PIDH.

CMEBJMVZ 30:18—19

Clue: T = W

DJAGPO, C TAJR BGH F KBTSJIB; RJ TAFPP VGS FPP TPJJL, DHS RJ

TAFPP FPP DJ WAFVYJO, CV F KGKJVS, CV SAJ SRCVEPCVY GM

FV JBJ, FS SAJ PFTS SIHKL: MGI SAJ SIHKLJS TAFPP TGHVO, FVO

SAJ OJFO TAFPP DJ IFCTJO CVWGIIHLSCDPJ, FVO RJ TAFPP DJ

WAFVYJO.

1 WGICVSACFVT 15:51—52

Clue: S = T

VICTORY!

ABRMR MBEII KETR GEZ GFAB ABR IEKC, EOH ABR IEKC MBEII

LDRZSLKR ABRK: JLZ BR FM ILZH LJ ILZHM, EOH TFOW LJ

TFOWM: EOH ABRX ABEA EZR GFAB BFK EZR SEIIRH, EOH

SBLMRO, EOH JEFABJNI.

ZRDRIEAFLO 17:14   *Clue: T = K*

YUMLM YUNCVL N UBKM LQWDMC PCYW FWP, YUBY NC TM

FM TNVUY UBKM QMBOM. NC YUM RWIZH FM LUBZZ UBKM

YINAPZBYNWC: APY AM WS VWWH OUMMI; N UBKM WKMIOWTM

YUM RWIZH.

XWUC 16:33   *Clue: T = M*

THE PATRIARCHS, PART 1

GSTCNSM ENYPP CND GYFS YGD FJMS LS QYPPSA YLMYF, LKC

CND GYFS ENYPP LS YLMYNYF; VJM Y VYCNSM JV FYGD GYCTJGE

NYBS T FYAS CNSS.

ISGSETE 17:5

Clue: G = N

C NR JES HUW UP NZYNENR JET PNJESY: PSNY LUJ, PUY C

NR GCJE JESS, NLW GCMM ZMSFF JESS, NLW RAMJCKMT JET

FSSW PUY RT FSYQNLJ NZYNENR'F FNOS. NLW ES ZACMWSW NL

NMJNY JESYS, NLW BNMMSW AKUL JES LNRS UP JES MUYW, NLW

KCJBESW ECF JSLJ JESYS.

HSLSFCF 26:24–25

Clue: C = I

THE PATRIARCHS, PART2

EUJVGX, K JOSU TUI IJU GOFX EURVAU DVM: YV KF OFX HVTTUTT IJU GOFX PJKZJ IJU GVAX TPOAU MFIV DVMA ROIJUAT, OEAOJOW, KTOOZ, OFX NOZVE, IV YKSU MFIV IJUW OFX IV IJUKA TUUX ORIUA IJUW.

XUMIUAVFVWD 1:8

Clue: E = B

YHP EYDCL GCFSP Y GCF, OYBTHU, TV UCP FTII LS FTKW RS, YHP FTII QSSA RS TH KWTO FYB KWYK T UC, YHP FTII UTGS RS LNSYP KC SYK, YHP NYTRSHK KC AMK CH, OC KWYK T DCRS YUYTH KC RB VYKWSN'O WCMOS TH ASYDS; KWSH OWYII KWS ICNP LS RB UCP

USHSOTO 28:20—21

Clue: U = G

FES, NMDXZS, JDMIM PFBM F WIMFJ HYES CIXB JDM HYZSMIEMTT,

FES TBXJM JDM CXRI PXIEMIT XC JDM DXRTM, FES YJ CMZZ ROXE

JDM GXREW BME, FES JDMG FIM SMFS; FES Y XEZG FB MTPFOMS

FZXEM JX JMZZ JDMM.

VXN 1:19   *Clue: J = T*

WLVEJH, AVL JECH SODDLH WU, OKH O BCLOA OKH DACEKB

ZNKH CLKA AVL XEGKAONKD, OKH WCOML NK SNLPLD AVL

CEPMD WLQECL AVL JECH; WGA AVL JECH ZOD KEA NK AVL

ZNKH: OKH OQALC AVL ZNKH OK LOCAVYGOML; WGA AVL JECH

ZOD KEA NK AVL LOCAVYGOML.

1 MNKBD 19:11   *Clue: D = S*

RAISED FROM THE DEAD

WMV QRVRF QMV VLRY ESS GJFVL, EHC AHRRSRC CJKH, EHC

QFEPRC; EHC VMFHZHU LZY VJ VLR WJCP IEZC, VEWZVLE, EFZIR.

EHC ILR JQRHRC LRF RPRI: EHC KLRH ILR IEK QRVRF, ILR IEV MQ.

EHC LR UEBR LRF LZI LEHC, EHC SZGVRC LRF MQ, EHC KLRH LR

LEC OESSRC VLR IEZHVI EHC KZCJKI, QFRIRHVRC LRF ESZBR.

EOVI 9:40–41   *Clue: K = W*

FEG FI JFCN XFI NREQ JVPFSOHEQ, OP ICEZ GRXE XHUO INPPJ,

FEG KPNN GRXE KVRA UOP UOHVG NRKU, FEG XFI UFZPE CJ

GPFG. FEG JFCN XPEU GRXE, FEG KPNN RE OHA, FEG PALVFSHEQ

OHA IFHG, UVRCLNP ERU BRCVIPNYPI; KRV OHI NHKP HI HE OHA.

FSUI 20:9–10   *Clue: J = P*

TAKING AN OFFERING

MJMHP XLR LNNBHTURA LI ZM VGHVBIMFZ UR ZUI ZMLHF, IB

OMF ZUX AUJM; RBF AHGTAURAOP, BH BC RMNMIIUFP: CBH ABT

OBJMFZ L NZMMHCGO AUJMH.

2 NBHURFZULRI 9:7 *Clue: J = V*

LPRAH BO JKK FIO FRFIOG RAFQ FIO GFQPOIQZGO, FIJF FIOPO

DJB LO DOJF RA DRAO IQZGO, JAV EPQWO DO AQT IOPOTRFI,

GJRFI FIO KQPV QM IQGFG, RM R TRKK AQF QEOA BQZ FIO

TRAVQTG QM IOJWOA, JAV EQZP BQZ QZF J LKOGGRAH, FIJF

FIOPO GIJKK AQF LO PQQD OAQZHI FQ POUORWO RF.

DJKJUIR 3:10 *Clue: D = M*

QUOTABLE EZRA

IBB VJGA IV AIL VTXIKIRTL RATQVTBMTV JFRS RATQ HKSQ RAT

HOBRAOFTVV SH RAT ATIRATF SH RAT BIFL, RS VTTW RAT BSKL

NSL SH OVKITB, LOL TIR, IFL WTXR RAT HTIVR SH JFBTIMTFTL

ZKTIL VTMTF LIDV PORA YSD.

TCKI 6:21–22   *Clue: G = C*

GXB VYZN JR BKP LUTPOBO YZA CPHTBPO YZA IKTPR JR BKP

RYBKPUO, DKJ DPUP YZITPZB VPZ, BKYB KYA OPPZ BKP RTUOB

KJXOP, DKPZ BKP RJXZAYBTJZ JR BKTO KJXOP DYO CYTA GPRJUP

BKPTU PNPO, DPLB DTBK Y CJXA HJTIP; YZA VYZN OKJXBPA YCJXA

RJU SJN: OJ BKYB BKP LPJLCP IJXCA ZJB ATOIPUZ BKP ZJTOP JR

BKP OKJXB JR SJN RUJV BKP ZJTOP JR BKP DPPLTZM JR BKP LPJLCP.

PEUY 3:12–13   *Clue: B = T*

TROUBLEMAKERS

LFX MUBJB SLH FY SLMBJ WYJ MUB ZYFOJBOLMAYF: LFX MUBE

OLMUBJBX MUBNHBTKBH MYOBMUBJ LOLAFHM NYHBH LFX

LOLAFHM LLJYF. LFX MUB IBYITB ZUYXB SAMU NYHBH, LFX HILPB,

HLEAFO, SYGTX OYX MULM SB ULX XABX SUBF YGJ RJBMUJBF

XABX RBWYJB MUB TYJX!

FGNRBJH 20:2–3   *Clue: O = G*

EKS OUI IEPOU RHIKIS UIP TRFOU, EKS QYEAARYIS OUIT FH

ORNIOUIP YMOU WRPEU, YUIK OUEO VRTHEKC SMIS, YUEO OMTI

OUI LMPI SIZRFPIS OYR UFKSPIS EKS LMLOC TIK: EKS OUIC DIVETI

E QMNK.

KFTDIPQ 26:10   *Clue: Q = S*

SQI RUTQ BUSPP SMMTSV RUT BKFQ XC RUT BXQ XC OSQ KQ

UTSGTQ: SQI RUTQ BUSPP SPP RUT RVKATB XC RUT TSVRU OXEVQ,

SQI RUTW BUSPP BTT RUT BXQ XC OSQ ZXOKQF KQ RUT ZPXEIB

XC UTSGTQ LKRU MXLTV SQI FVTSR FPXVW.

OSRRUTL 24:30   *Clue: O = M*

SZD HI DYKD VKW KCV DYKD YHZP TCHAUDY CH FKC, CH, CHD

DYU KCJUOL AYBRY KPU BC YUKEUC, CUBDYUP DYU LHC, SZD

DYU IKDYUP. DKTU WU YUUV, AKDRY KCV QPKW: IHP WU TCHA

CHD AYUC DYU DBFU BL.

FKPT 13:32—33   *Clue: T = K*

A COMMON WOMAN'S NAME

ZA TWG GIZA GIL SMEQLTGLE'A AWT? ZA TWG IZA NWGILE

SMFFLB NMEO? MTB IZA CELGIELT, KMNLA, MTB KWALA, MTB

AZNWT, MTB KDBMA?

NMGGILR 13:55   *Clue: E = R*

TCE MPUC GPU ITAATGP MTI XTIG, RTNH RTBETFUCU, TCE RTNH

GPU RKGPUN KL QTRUI, TCE ITFKRU, PTE AKYBPG IMUUG IXDJUI,

GPTG GPUH RDBPG JKRU TCE TCKDCG PDR.

RTNO 16:1   *Clue: R = M*

EGMFBHKT YPK WBWBKF PGC YPKD QTGC: YPKD YGBW MGY,

YPKD FXBM MGY; IMH DKY B FID SMYG DGS, YPIY FGWGUGM BM

IWW PBF QWGTD CIF MGY ITTIDKH WBAK GMK GV YPKFK.

WSAK 12:27   *Clue: F = S*

V KSTG LGGA JICAF, SAO AIN SQ IUO; JGP KSTG V AIP MGGA

PKG WVFKPGICM BIWMSXGA, AIW KVM MGGO LGFFVAF LWGSO.

DMSUQ 37:25   *Clue: W = R*

IMPORTANT QUESTIONS

QLNB DL RTI, RLAIMLB HL NQBNAO: MNUL RTI A ITPO IMLL

QBTW IMNI IAWL, NRO MNUL OLJPNBLO AI? DL NBL LULR WD

YAIRLZZLZ. AZ IMLBL N STO HLZAOL WL? DLN, IMLBL AZ RT STO;

A XRTY RTI NRD.

AZNANM 44:8 _Clue: D = Y_

ZRS VUFO SUF DUNCYBFFB UNE UFNCE SUNS UF UNE DRS SUF

BNEERMFFB SW BYQFOMF, SUFH VFCF XNSUFCFE SWXFSUFC.

SUFO WOF WK SUFT, VUYMU VNB N QNVHFC, NBPFE UYT N

LRFBSYWO, SFTDSYOX UYT, NOE BNHYOX, TNBSFC, VUYMU YB SUF

XCFNS MWTTNOETFOS YO SUF QNV?

TNSSUFV 22:34—36 _Clue: V = W_

176

MARTYRS

EPW OLHQ IOSPHW IOHGLHP, MEYYAPB DGSP BSW, EPW IEQAPB,

YSTW NHIDI, THMHAFH XQ IGATAO. EPW LH UPHHYHW WSRP, EPW

MTAHW RAOL E YSDW FSAMH, YSTW, YEQ PSO OLAI IAP OS

OLHAT MLETBH. EPW RLHP LH LEW IEAW OLAI, LH CHYY EIYHHG.

EMOI 7:59—60   *Clue: Y = L*

PDGT UGHG QPJWGF, PDGT UGHG QEUW EQNWFGH, UGHG

PGVZPGF, UGHG QBECW UCPD PDG QUJHF: PDGT UEWFGHGF

EYJNP CW QDGGZQSCWQ EWF RJEPQSCWQ; YGCWR FGQPCPNPG,

EMMBCLPGF, PJHVGWPGF; (JM UDJV PDG UJHBF UEQ WJP

UJHPDT).

DGYHGUQ 11:37—38   *Clue: E = A*

MAH WEMYMTE NMQH OAPT FTNDWE, Q EMGD HYDMKDH M

HYDMK, MAH PEDYD QN ATAD PEMP UMA QAPDYWYDP QP: MAH

Q EMGD EDMYH NMB TC PEDD, PEMP PETO UMANP OAHDYNPMAH

M HYDMK PT QAPDYWYDP QP.

JDADNQN 41:15   *Clue: W = P*

TMU FA PSQU GP PS FGJ KTPFAB, TMU PS FGJ CBAPFBAM: TMU

FGJ KTPFAB BACWDAU FGV, TMU JTGU WMPS FGV, NFTP GJ PFGJ

UBATV PFTP PFSW FTJP UBATVAU? JFTQQ G TMU PFR VSPFAB

TMU PFR CBAPFBAM GMUAAU LSVA PS CSN USNM SWBJAQZAJ PS

PFAA PS PFA ATBPF?

OAMAJGJ 37:10   *Clue: C = B*

A WORD FROM AMOS

UGS, VG, OL IORI UGSYLIO IOL YGDAIRBAJ, RAK ZSLRILIO IOL FBAK,

RAK KLZVRSLIO DAIG YRA FORI BJ OBJ IOGDEOI, IORI YRPLIO IOL

YGSABAE KRSPALJJ, RAK ISLRKLIO DMGA IOL OBEO MVRZLJ GU IOL

LRSIO, IOL VGSK, IOL EGK GU OGJIJ, BJ OBJ ARYL.

RYGJ 4:13

Clue: K = D

OBTSTVMST OBT VKEWBO FBRKK YTSEFB VSMI OBT FUEVO, RGC

OBT FOSMGW FBRKK GMO FOSTGWOBTG BEF VMSQT, GTEOBTS

FBRKK OBT IEWBOA CTKEXTS BEIFTKV: GTEOBTS FBRKK BT FORGC

OBRO BRGCKTOB OBT LMU; RGC BT OBRO EF FUEVO MV VMMO

FBRKK GMO CTKEXTS BEIFTKV: GTEOBTS FBRKK BT OBRO SECTOB

OBT BMSFT CTKEXTS BEIFTKV.

RIMF 2:14–15

Clue: V = F

THE OPPOSITE OF PROUD

FIDUBDSQDJFCBFY SKEKMBJS SHRPGKC SBRQKGT TIZ DSK AZBCK IT SBQ SKJZD, PIDS SK JFC DSK BFSJPBDJFDQ IT NKZHQJGKR, QI DSJD DSK UZJDS IT DSK GIZC VJRK FID HAIF DSKR BF DSK CJWQ IT SKEKMBJS.

2 VSZIFBVGKQ 32:26 *Clue: G = L*

SVDL RPS HERPIZ FCSV SVI FDPZH DW SVB GDLSV, SVDL RPS SRAIE FCSV SVI FDPZH DW SVB GDLSV. ZD SVCH EDF, GB HDE, REZ ZIKCTIP SVBHIKW, FVIE SVDL RPS MDGI CESD SVI VREZ DW SVB WPCIEZ; XD, VLGNKI SVBHIKW, REZ GRAI HLPI SVB WPCIEZ.

YPDTIPNH 6:2–3 *Clue: L = U*

GUILTY!

KAT TS NKAT DOJD TOJD DOCKPR RASXSG DOS VJT RJCDO, CD
RJCDO DA DOSY TOA JGS IKMSG DOS VJT: DOJD SXSGB YAIDO
YJB ES RDAFFSM, JKM JVV DOS TAGVM YJB ESLAYS PICVDB
ESUAGS PAM.

GAYJKR 3:19

Clue: V = L

OKE FN JH GSZH LHMUHIE ER UHLMRTM, JH IRBBFE MFT,
STW SLH IRTZFTIHW RN EGH CSV SM ELSTMQLHMMRLM. NRL
VGRMRHZHL MGSCC AHHU EGH VGRCH CSV, STW JHE RNNHTW
FT RTH URFTE, GH FM QKFCEJ RN SCC.

PSBHM 2:9–10

Clue: R = O

FORGIVEN!

OSG LE AMF MFLQFH WE MWUM LPSQF AMF FLGAM, ES UGFLA

WE MWE CFGKR ASTLGY AMFC AMLA OFLG MWC. LE OLG LE

AMF FLEA WE OGSC AMF TFEA, ES OLG MLAM MF GFCSQFY SBG

AGLHEUGFEEWSHE OGSC BE.

VELIC 103:11–12   *Clue: A = T*

GT CS YUL HAUH CS AUNS TSIIBCYAGF CGHA AGP, UER CUIW GE

RUOWESYY, CS IGS, UER RB EBH HAS HOZHA: VZH GT CS CUIW

GE HAS IGMAH, UY AS GY GE HAS IGMAH, CS AUNS TSIIBCYAGF

BES CGHA UEBHASO, UER HAS VIBBR BT KSYZY DAOGYH AGY YBE

DISUEYSHA ZY TOBP UII YGE.

1 KBAE 1:6–7   *Clue: S = E*

GOSSIP AND SLANDER

IJH M IDRH, TDGY, SCDB M AJXD, M GCRTT BJY IMBL EJO GOAC

RG M SJOTL, RBL YCRY M GCRTT UD IJOBL OBYJ EJO GOAC RG

ED SJOTL BJY: TDGY YCDHD UD LDURYDG, DBNEMBPG, SHRYCG,

GYHMIDG, URAQUMYMBPG, SCMGZDHMBPG, GSDTTMBPG, YOXOTYG.

2 AJHMBYCMRBG 12:20   *Clue: I = F*

HLJB, PML AMNHH NKSBD SR CMI CNKDJRNOHD? PML AMNHH

BPDHH SR CMI MLHI MSHH? MD CMNC PNHFDCM ETJSZMCHI, NRB

PLJFDCM JSZMCDLEARDAA, NRB ATDNFDCM CMD CJECM SR MSA

MDNJC. MD CMNC KNOFKSCDCM RLC PSCM MSA CLRZED, RLJ

BLDCM DWSH CL MSA RDSZMKLEJ.

TANHV 15:1–3   *Clue: P = W*

AHC PA FDP DPQ LBZPO, XEL LA GAYC APC DPALBCT: SAT BC

LBDL GAYCLB DPALBCT BDLB SEGSZGGCR LBC GDH.

TAFDPI 13:8   *Clue: L = T*

CNNSOY RN QEJN TABSHSNU RGAB CGADC SO GKNRSOY MQN

MBAMQ MQBGAYQ MQN CTSBSM AOMG AOHNSYONU DGJN GH

MQN KBNMQBNO, CNN MQEM RN DGJN GON EOGMQNB ISMQ

E TABN QNEBM HNBJNOMDR: KNSOY KGBO EYESO, OGM GH

LGBBATMSKDN CNNU, KAM GH SOLGBBATMSKDN, KR MQN IGBU

GH YGU.

1 TNMNB 1:22—23   *Clue: E = A*

BIBLICAL SKYSCRAPERS

MW IOMGL LRKOILLU, PYMU EOMJ IOL IMELW RU GRBMCJ HLBB,

CUF GBLE IOLJ, IORUN DL IOCI IOLD ELWL GRUULWG CAMZL CBB

JLU IOCI FELBI RU SLWPGCBLJ? R ILBB DMP, UCD: API, LTVLYI DL

WLYLUI, DL GOCBB CBB BRNLERGL YLWRGO.

BPNL 13:4–5

Clue: D = Y

RU CU, SNC HT POLN IAMDL, OGF IHAG CENP CEUAUHRESB. OGF

CENB EOF IAMDL WUA TCUGN, OGF TSMPN EOF CENB WUA

PUACNA. OGF CENB TOMF, RU CU, SNC HT IHMSF HT O DMCB

OGF O CUXNA, XEUTN CUZ POB ANODE HGCU ENOJNG; OGF

SNC HT POLN HT O GOPN, SNTC XN IN TDOCCNANF OIAUOF.

RNGNTMT 11:3–4

Clue: F = D

LSLU DK PEBNG, BP BN GENG UKN FKJOD, BD ALEA, HLBUM

ERKUL. TLE, E CEU CET DET, NGKI GEDN PEBNG, EUA B GESL

FKJOD: DGLF CL NGT PEBNG FBNGKIN NGT FKJOD, EUA B FBRR

DGLF NGLL CT PEBNG HT CT FKJOD.

VECLD 2:17–18   *Clue: C = M*

KILT VRGBDG DLTG VHIO HBC KFZRSFBZO HTLBZ ALN? DLTG SRGA

BLS RGBDG, GUGB LK ALNI MNOSO SRHS VHI FB ALNI TGTEGIO?

AG MNOS, HBC RHUG BLS: AG PFMM, HBC CGOFIG SL RHUG,

HBC DHBBLS LESHFB: AG KFZRS HBC VHI, AGS AG RHUG BLS,

EGDHNOG AG HOP BLS.

QHTGO 4:1–2   *Clue: D = C*

MORE ADVICE FROM JAMES

EJPUPGO NP VHLE HLF EJGF OJGQQ KP LH FJP SLUULE. MLU

EJGF AO NLYU QAMP? AF AO PWPH G WGBLYU, FJGF GBBPGUPFJ

MLU G QAFFQP FASP, GHI FJPH WGHAOJPFJ GEGN. MLU FJGF NP

LYCJF FL OGN, AM FJP QLUI EAQQ, EP OJGQQ QAWP, GHI IL FJAO,

LU FJGF.

TGSPO 4:14–15   *Clue: L = O*

IB LSNUBEN NJBVBOTVB, IVBNJVBE, KENT NJB YTRUEF TO NJB ZTVH.

IBJTZH, NJB JKPISEHRSE QSUNBNJ OTV NJB LVBYUTKP OVKUN TO

NJB BSVNJ, SEH JSNJ ZTEF LSNUBEYB OTV UN, KENUZ JB VBYBUAB

NJB BSVZC SEH ZSNNBV VSUE. IB CB SZPT LSNUBEN; PNSIZUPJ CTKV

JBSVNP: OTV NJB YTRUEF TO NJB ZTVH HVSQBNJ EUFJ.

MSRBP 5:7–8   *Clue: I = B*

FPMD CTNFP PM FG FPGSTC, KMTLP PNFPMK FPB HNDYMK, TDA

WMPGJA SB PTDAC; TDA KMTLP PNFPMK FPB PTDA, TDA FPKECF

NF NDFG SB CNAM: TDA WM DGF HTNFPJMCC, WEF WMJNMUNDY.

OGPD 20:27   *Clue: C = S*

MCFNF FHOUB NLUE BOS, UBESHF, ACIHNFC UBEN BHFU FCCL

SC, UBEN BHFU ACJOCDCK: AJCFFCK HGC UBCT UBHU BHDC LEU

FCCL, HLK TCU BHDC ACJOCDCK.

MEBL 20:29   *Clue: A = B*

TRUE MOTIVATION

KUF IRKEDTCSCW NC FT AU ITWF TW FCCF, FT KHH AU ERC UKGC TP ERC HTWF VCDLD, OASAUO ERKUYD ET OTF KUF ERC PKERCW ZN RAG.

JTHTDDAKUD 3:17   *Clue: R = H*

DVA AECV, C PNK CT SCZ, TUBB AEBWB AEJKSW; NKZ TCUUCO NTABL LJSEABCVWKBWW, SCZUJKBWW, TNJAE, UCMB, GNAJBKFB, PBBIKBWW.

1 AJPCAEX 6:11   *Clue: S = G*

A BIBLICAL QUEEN

CPL NTHP UTH YMHHP KS FTHEC THCBL KS UTH SCDH KS

FKZKDKP GKPGHBPOPI UTH PCDH KS UTH ZKBL, FTH GCDH UK

JBKRH TOD NOUT TCBL YMHFUOKPF.

1 AOPIF 10:1   *Clue: F = S*

KAB OFBBL TR KAB UTFKA UAQCC GSUB FV SL KAB NFZEPBLK

DSKA KAB PBL TR KASU EBLBGQKSTL, QLZ JTLZBPL KABP: RTG

UAB JQPB RGTP KAB FKPTUK VQGKU TR KAB BQGKA KT ABQG

KAB DSUZTP TR UTCTPTL; QLZ, YBATCZ, Q EGBQKBG KAQL

UTCTPTL SU ABGB.

CFWB 11:31   *Clue: G = R*

TREES

RGO FUJN UJRLO FUJ ISCMJ SB FUJ ASLO HSO DRAECGH CG FUJ

HRLOJG CG FUJ MSSA SB FUJ ORN: RGO RORV RGO UCP DCBJ

UCO FUJVPJAIJP BLSV FUJ YLJPJGMJ SB FUJ ASLO HSO RVSGHPF

FUJ FLJJP SB FUJ HRLOJG.

HJGJPCP 3:8

Clue: A = L

FAED RAMBF KEF UBMKF FASS M NOELS EH MKJ FOSSR KSMO

DKFE FAS MBFMO EH FAS BEOY FAJ NEY, CAPTA FAED RAMBF

ZMVS FASS.

YSDFSOEKEZJ 16:21

Clue: D = U

WHEN LIFE DOESN'T MAKE SENSE

HAO YP BLASVLBI GOT FAB PASO BLASVLBI, FTUBLTO GOT PASO

KGPI YP KGPI, IGUBL BLT EAON. HAO GI BLT LTGZTFI GOT LUVLTO

BLGF BLT TGOBL, IA GOT YP KGPI LUVLTO BLGF PASO KGPI, GFN

YP BLASVLBI BLGF PASO BLASVLBI.

UIGUGL 55:8–9   *Clue: T = E*

REAS UHT ISJKANAY REA DHNY, ISY JIGY, G VSHK REIR REHM FISJR

YH AOANB REGSC, ISY REIR SH REHMCER FIS TA KGREEHDYAS

PNHQ REAA. KEH GJ EA REIR EGYARE FHMSJAD KGREHMR

VSHKDAYCA? REANAPHNA EIOA G MRRANAY REIR G MSYANJRHHY

SHR; REGSCJ RHH KHSYANPMD PHN QA, KEGFE G VSAK SHR.

UHT 42:1–3   *Clue: G = I*

ROCK AND ROLL

OTCGC WABBSNT P KAN GTPMM EPMM NTSJSAH: PHW TS NTPN

JCMMSNT P GNCHS, AN OAMM JSNLJH LKCH TAI.

KJCUSJXG 26:27   *Clue: C = O*

KAR, GNUBXR, SUNVN JKM K CVNKS NKVSUHOKTN: PBV SUN

KACNX BP SUN XBVR RNMENARNR PVBI UNKWNA, KAR EKIN KAR

VBXXNR GKET SUN MSBAN PVBI SUN RBBV, KAR MKS ODBA FS.

IKSSUNJ 28:2   *Clue: R = D*

WHAT A WASTE. . .

KLBFOR AT KLBFOFUI, ILFOE OEU HCULMEUC, KLBFOR AT

KLBFOFUI; LPP FI KLBFOR. VELO HCATFO ELOE L JLB AT LPP EFI

PLDASC VEFME EU OLXUOE SBGUC OEU ISB?

UMMPUIFLIOUI 1:2–3   *Clue: A = O*

NIA PORE HC R LRU WAINHEJG, HN OJ CORSS FRHU EOJ POISJ

PIASG, RUG SICJ OHC IPU CIQS? IA PORE CORSS R LRU FHKJ HU

JBMORUFJ NIA OHC CIQS?

LREEOJP 16:26   *Clue: F = G*

GIMME A SIGN

TCB GWDFLC VPFGGFB NOFD, TCB GTWB MCNL DTJE OWG

DLNOFJ, VFOLPB, NOWG IOWPB WG GFN KLJ NOF KTPP TCB

JWGWCS TSTWC LK DTCE WC WGJTFP; TCB KLJ T GWSC AOWIO

GOTPP VF GRLHFC TSTWCGN.

PMHF 2:34   *Clue: J = R*

LRF MB ICTVBABN ICN TISN RCFD FMBH, IC BXSE ICN INREFBADRT

JBCBAIFSDC TBBPBFM IGFBA I TSJC; ICN FMBAB TMIEE CD TSJC

LB JSXBC FD SF, LRF FMB TSJC DG FMB KADKMBF UDCIT.

HIFFMBV 12:39   *Clue: L = B*

LABPDT ITA LDPNRIGPAL; CEP NO ITAH MA ITNOX MA TBSA

AIAPOBJ JNCA: BOU ITAM BPA ITAM YTNDT IALINCM EC HA.

VETO 5:39   *Clue: T = H*

BRH DLJ NMJDLMJR CUUJHCBDJEA FJRD BQBA SBPE BRH FCEBF

NA RCKLD PRDI NJMJB: QLI TIUCRK DLCDLJM QJRD CRDI DLJ

FARBKIKPJ IO DLJ GJQF. DLJFJ QJMJ UIMJ RINEJ DLBR DLIFJ CR

DLJFFBEIRCTB, CR DLBD DLJA MJTJCXJH DLJ QIMH QCDL BEE

MJBHCRJFF IO UCRH, BRH FJBMTLJH DLJ FTMCSDPMJF HBCEA.

BTDF 17:10–11   *Clue: H = D*

GOD'S WEALTH

BEA PRSJAH RP LRFA, UFK BEA CGSK RP LRFA, PURBE BEA SGHK
GD EGPBP.

EUCCUR 2:8

Clue: P = S

GDN AJANO MAHBP DG PIA GDNABP UB XURA, HRC PIA THPPQA

EZDR H PIDEBHRC IUQQB. U LRDS HQQ PIA GDSQB DG PIA

XDERPHURB: HRC PIA SUQC MAHBPB DG PIA GUAQC HNA XURA.

UG U SANA IERVNO, U SDEQC RDP PAQQ PIAA: GDN PIA SDNQC

UB XURA, HRC PIA GEQRABB PIANADG.

ZBHQX 50:10–12

Clue: X = M

IOM NCPGP IAP NCPL ECTZC LP GCIBB CISP TO IVFHTOINTFO IHFOK NCP UFEBG; NCPL GCIBB OFN VP PINPO, NCPL IAP IO IVFHTOINTFO: NCP PIKBP, IOM NCP FGGTUAIKP, IOM NCP FGDAIL.

BPSTNTZYG 11:13   *Clue: V = B*

Y FYEE DYKC MRCC VPMS MRC IHKCPSVO LYIGO SJ CKCIQ OSIM, HPG MS MRC LCHOMO SJ MRC JYCEG MS LC GCKSVICG.

CXCUYCE 39:4   *Clue: L = B*

NICE BIRDS

LAW FSM MOS DULAASOD DSRN YSA L YLAMVEFB? LFN SFW

SY MVWC DVLRR FSM YLRR SF MVW BASPFN OEMVSPM HSPA

YLMVWA.

CLMMVWO 10:29   *Clue: U = P*

UCF AHSRFEK DLLFDE ST UCF FDEUC; UCF UPBF SA UCF KPTXPTX

SA JPEYK PK OSBF, DTY UCF MSPOF SA UCF UWEUHF PK CFDEY

PT SWE HDTY.

KSTX SA KSHSBST 2:12   *Clue: H = L*

KRL SU MO PSU IHTIMPMKPMTR ATH TGH OMRO: KRL RTP ATH

TGHO TRBF, EGP KBOT ATH PSU OMRO TA PSU JSTBU JTHBL.

1 NTSR 2:2   *Clue: M = I*

CXE CLA POWQSOHOP GEH EJH EGGOIBOA, LIP CLA HLQAOP

LFLQI GEH EJH RJAKQGQBLKQEI.

HEDLIA 4:25   *Clue: I = N*

UC PHDAR NTLEO OTHM TRLI DK OTR UHIKDKB, H EHIF; DK OTR UHIKDKB GDEE D FDIRAO UC SILCRI MKOH OTRR, LKF GDEE EHHX MS.

SNLEU 5:3   *Clue: C = Y*

LBR CSPJEWEPR TW LBR AEPQRF EC SO SNTHEOSLETO LT LBR DTJF: NIL LBR GJSXRJ TW LBR IGJEKBL EC BEC FRDEKBL.

GJTMRJNC 15:8   *Clue: F = D*

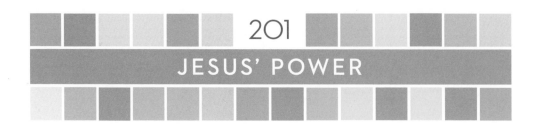

JESUS' POWER

CGG FMJOIH QYAY RAYCFYU SB MJP, COU TEA MJP: COU MY JH

SYTEAY CGG FMJOIH, COU SB MJP CGG FMJOIH REOHJHF.

REGEHHJCOH 1:16–17   *Clue: E = O*

PEGP GP PEN DGON LK BNIAI NUNHR QDNN IELASV FLC, LK

PEMDJI MD ENGUND, GDV PEMDJI MD NGHPE, GDV PEMDJI ADVNH

PEN NGHPE.

TEMSMTTMGDI 2:10   *Clue: L = O*

GASU OTWBU DSGSY JUOHSYSI ATW, FBYI, GB HABW OAJFF HS

EB? GABM AJOG GAS HBYIO BV SGSYUJF FTVS.

KBAU 6:68   *Clue: H = W*

JSCY QFHJ RSAQ UA JSA BNJS CP HFPA: FM JST BDARAMIA FR

PYHMARR CP OCT; NJ JST DFLSJ SNME JSADA NDA BHANRYDAR

PCD AKADUCDA.

BRNHU 16:11   *Clue: F = I*

BIBLE CRYPTOGRAMS ANSWER KEY

1) Born Again!

For I am not ashamed of the gospel of Christ: for it is the power of God unto salvation to every one that believeth; to the Jew first, and also to the Greek. ROMANS 1:16

But we are bound to give thanks alway to God for you, brethren beloved of the Lord, because God hath from the beginning chosen you to salvation through sanctification of the Spirit and belief of the truth. 2 THESSALONIANS 2:13

2) The Key Ingredient

And Jesus said unto him, Go thy way; thy faith hath made thee whole. And immediately he received his sight, and followed Jesus in the way. MARK 10:52

For therein is the righteousness of God revealed from faith to faith: as it is written, The just shall live by faith. ROMANS 1:17

3) A Wing and a Prayer

Our soul is escaped as a bird out of the snare of the fowlers: the snare is broken, and we are escaped. PSALM 124:7

Curse not the king, no not in thy thought; and curse not the rich in thy bedchamber: for a bird of the air shall carry the voice, and that which hath wings shall tell the matter. ECCLESIASTES 10:20

4) A Very Important Person

And the child grew, and she brought him unto Pharaoh's daughter, and he became her son. And she called his name Moses: and she said, Because I drew him out of the water. EXODUS 2:10

By faith Moses, when he was come to years, refused to be called the son of Pharaoh's daughter; choosing rather to suffer affliction with the people of God, than to enjoy the pleasures of sin for a season. HEBREWS 11:24–25

5) Keep Looking Up

Behold, the eye of the LORD is upon them that fear him, upon them that hope in his mercy. PSALM 33:18

Blessed be the God and Father of our Lord Jesus Christ, which according to his abundant mercy hath begotten us again unto a lively hope by the resurrection of Jesus Christ from the dead. 1 PETER 1:3

6) Lives Changed

Now when they saw the boldness of Peter and John, and perceived that they were unlearned and ignorant men, they marvelled; and they took knowledge of them, that they had been with Jesus. ACTS 4:13

And Zacchaeus stood, and said unto the Lord: Behold, Lord, the half of my goods I give to the poor; and if I have taken any thing from any man by false accusation, I restore him fourfold. And Jesus said unto him, This day is salvation come to this house. LUKE 19:8–9

7) Powerful Stuff

My soul cleaveth unto the dust: quicken thou me according to thy word. PSALM 119:25

For the word of God is quick, and powerful, and sharper than any twoedged sword, piercing even to the dividing asunder of soul and spirit, and of the joints and marrow, and is a discerner of the thoughts and intents of the heart. HEBREWS 4:12

8) Good Kings

And thus did Hezekiah throughout all Judah, and wrought that which was good and right and truth before the LORD his God. 2 CHRONICLES 31:20

And Josiah took away all the abominations out of all the countries that pertained to the children of Israel, and made all that were present in Israel to serve, even to serve the LORD their God. 2 CHRONICLES 34:33

9) Bad Kings

But he did that which was evil in the sight of the LORD, as did Manasseh his father: for Amon sacrificed unto all the carved images which Manasseh his father had made, and served them. 2 CHRONICLES 33:22

And Ahab the son of Omri did evil in the sight of the LORD above all that were before him. 1 KINGS 16:30

10) Spiritual Fruit

Even so every good tree bringeth forth good fruit; but a corrupt tree bringeth forth evil fruit. MATTHEW 7:17

But now being made free from sin, and become servants to God, ye have your fruit unto holiness, and the end everlasting life. ROMANS 6:22

11) Simon Says

And Simon Peter answered and said, Thou art the Christ, the Son of the living God. MATTHEW 16:16

Peter said unto him, Lord, why cannot I follow thee now? I will lay down my life for thy sake. JOHN 13:37

12) The Flood

And God said unto Noah, The end of all flesh is come before me; for the earth is filled with violence through them; and, behold, I will destroy them with the earth. GENESIS 6:13

And Noah did according unto all that the LORD commanded him. GENESIS 7:5

13) Old Testament Miracles

And the LORD said unto Moses, Stretch out thine hand toward heaven, that there may be darkness over the land of

Egypt, even darkness which may be felt. Exodus 10:21

And it came to pass, as they were burying a man, that, behold, they spied a band of men; and they cast the man into the sepulchre of Elisha: and when the man was let down, and touched the bones of Elisha, he revived, and stood up on his feet. 2 Kings 13:21

14) The End of Time

And many of them that sleep in the dust of the earth shall awake, some to everlasting life, and some to shame and everlasting contempt. Daniel 12:2

And I saw a new heaven and a new earth: for the first heaven and the first earth were passed away; and there was no more sea. Revelation 21:1

15) Great Stuff from the Psalms

For the Lord knoweth the way of the righteous: but the way of the ungodly shall perish. Psalm 1:6

It is a good thing to give thanks unto the Lord, and to sing praises unto thy name, O Most High: to shew forth thy lovingkindness in the morning, and thy faithfulness every night. Psalm 92:1–2

16) More Great Stuff from the Psalms

There is a river, the streams whereof shall make glad the city of God, the holy place of the tabernacles of the most High. Psalm 46:4

Praise ye the Lord. Praise God in his sanctuary: praise him in the firmament of his power. Praise him for his mighty acts: praise him according to his excellent greatness. Psalm 150:1–2

17) John the Baptist

For I say unto you, Among those that are born of women there is not a greater prophet than John the Baptist: but he that is least in the kingdom of God is greater than he. Luke 7:28

For John the Baptist came neither eating bread nor drinking wine; and ye say, He hath a devil. The Son of man is come eating and drinking; and ye say, Behold a gluttonous man, and a winebibber, a friend of publicans and sinners! Luke 7:33–34

18) Precious Metals

Ye shall not make with me gods of silver, neither shall ye make unto you gods of gold. Exodus 20:23

And the twelve gates were twelve pearls: every several gate was of one pearl: and the street of the city was pure gold, as it were transparent glass. Revelation 21:21

19) Hey, Good Lookin'

But in all Israel there was none to be so much praised as Absalom for his beauty: from the sole of his foot even to the crown of his head there was no blemish in him. 2 Samuel 14:25

And he brought up Hadassah, that is, Esther, his uncle's daughter: for she had neither father nor mother, and the maid was fair and beautiful; whom Mordecai, when her father and mother were dead, took for his own daughter. Esther 2:7

20) Prophets in General

And he said, Hear now my words: If there be a prophet among you, I the Lord will make myself known unto him in a vision, and will speak unto him in a dream. Numbers 12:6

But the prophet, which shall presume to speak a word in my name, which I have not commanded him to speak, or that shall speak in the name of other gods, even that prophet shall die. Deuteronomy 18:20

21) Prophets in Specific

And they told the king, saying, Behold Nathan the prophet. And when he was come in before the king, he bowed himself before the king with his face to the ground. 1 Kings 1:23

How long halt ye between two opinions? if the Lord be God, follow him: but if Baal, then follow him. And the people answered him not a word. Then said Elijah unto the people, I, even I only, remain a prophet of the Lord; but Baal's prophets are four hundred and fifty men. 1 Kings 18:21–22

22) More Prophets in Specific

In those days was Hezekiah sick unto death. And Isaiah the prophet the son of Amoz came unto him, and said unto him, Thus saith the Lord, Set thine house in order: for thou shalt die, and not live. Isaiah 38:1

Even the prophet Jeremiah said, Amen: the Lord do so: the Lord perform thy words which thou hast prophesied, to bring again the vessels of the Lord's house, and all that is carried away captive, from Babylon into this place. Jeremiah 28:6

23) Key Ideas of the New Testament

Now there are diversities of gifts, but the same Spirit. And there are differences of administrations, but the same Lord. And there are diversities of operations, but it is the same God which worketh all in all. 1 Corinthians 12:4–6

And every priest standeth daily ministering and offering oftentimes the same sacrifices, which can never take away sins: But this man, after he had offered one sacrifice for sins for ever, sat down on the right hand of God. Hebrews 10:11–12

24) Cleanliness Is Next to Godliness

He shall therefore burn that garment, whether warp or woof, in woollen or in linen, or any thing of skin, wherein the plague is: for it is a fretting leprosy; it shall be burnt in the fire. Leviticus 13:52

And the leper in whom the plague is, his clothes shall be rent, and his head bare, and he shall put a covering upon his upper lip, and shall cry, Unclean, unclean. All the days wherein the plague shall be in him he shall be defiled; he is unclean: he shall dwell alone. LEVITICUS 13:45–46

25) Verses Worth Memorizing

But God commendeth his love toward us, in that, while we were yet sinners, Christ died for us. ROMANS 5:8

Be not deceived; God is not mocked: for whatsoever a man soweth, that shall he also reap. For he that soweth to his flesh shall of the flesh reap corruption; but he that soweth to the Spirit shall of the Spirit reap life everlasting. GALATIANS 6:7–8

26) Attributes of God

Now unto the King eternal, immortal, invisible, the only wise God, be honour and glory for ever and ever. Amen. 1 TIMOTHY 1:17

Then came the word of the LORD unto Jeremiah, saying, Behold, I am the LORD, the God of all flesh: is there any thing too hard for me? JEREMIAH 32:26–27

27) Real Smarts

The fear of the LORD is the beginning of wisdom: a good understanding have all they that do his commandments: his praise endureth for ever. PSALM 111:10

Wisdom is the principal thing; therefore get wisdom: and with all thy getting get understanding. PROVERBS 4:7

28) Jonah's Story

Arise, go to Nineveh, that great city, and cry against it; for their wickedness is come up before me. But Jonah rose up to flee unto Tarshish from the presence of the LORD, and went down

to Joppa. JONAH 1:2–3

I cried by reason of mine affliction unto the LORD, and he heard me; out of the belly of hell cried I, and thou heardest my voice. For thou hadst cast me into the deep, in the midst of the seas; and the floods compassed me about. JONAH 2:2–3

29) Lamentable

How hath the LORD covered the daughter of Zion with a cloud in his anger, and cast down from heaven unto the earth the beauty of Israel, and remembered not his footstool in the day of his anger! LAMENTATIONS 2:1

For the LORD will not cast off for ever: But though he cause grief, yet will he have compassion according to the multitude of his mercies. LAMENTATIONS 3:31–32

30) Parables of Jesus

And he spake a parable unto them, Can the blind lead the blind? shall they not both fall into the ditch? LUKE 6:39

The kingdom of heaven is like to a grain of mustard seed, which a man took, and sowed in his field: Which indeed is the least of all seeds: but when it is grown, it is the greatest among herbs, and becometh a tree, so that the birds of the air come and lodge in the branches thereof. MATTHEW 13:31–32

31) More Parables of Jesus

Another parable spake he unto them; The kingdom of heaven is like unto leaven, which a woman took, and hid in three measures of meal, till the whole was leavened. MATTHEW 13:33

Now learn a parable of the fig tree; When his branch is yet tender, and putteth forth leaves, ye know that summer is nigh: So likewise ye, when ye shall see all these things, know that it is near, even at the doors. MATTHEW 24:32–33

32) Jewelry in the Bible

And they came, both men and women, as many as were willing hearted, and brought bracelets, and earrings, and rings, and tablets, all jewels of gold: and every man that offered offered an offering of gold unto the LORD. EXODUS 35:22

In that day the Lord will take away the bravery of their tinkling ornaments about their feet. . .the chains, and the bracelets, and the mufflers, the bonnets, and the ornaments of the legs, and the headbands, and the tablets, and the earrings, the rings, and nose jewels. ISAIAH 3:18–21

33) Old Folks

And Lamech lived after he begat Noah five hundred ninety and five years, and begat sons and daughters: And all the days of Lamech were seven hundred seventy and seven years: and he died. GENESIS 5:30–31

And Methuselah lived an hundred eighty and seven years, and begat Lamech. And Methuselah lived after he begat Lamech seven hundred eighty and two years, and begat sons and daughters: And all the days of Methuselah were nine hundred sixty and nine years: and he died. GENESIS 5:25–27

34) Theology of Romans, Part 1

Therefore by the deeds of the law there shall no flesh be justified in his sight: for by the law is the knowledge of sin. ROMANS 3:20

For the invisible things of him from the creation of the world are clearly seen, being understood by the things that are made, even his eternal power and Godhead; so that they are without excuse: Because that, when they knew God, they glorified him not as God, neither were thankful; but became vain in their imaginations. ROMANS 1:20–21

35) Theology of Romans, Part 2

For if, when we were enemies, we were reconciled to God by the death of his Son, much more, being reconciled, we shall be saved by his life. ROMANS 5:10

There is therefore now no condemnation to them which are in Christ Jesus, who walk not after the flesh, but after the Spirit. For the law of the Spirit of life in Christ Jesus hath made me free from the law of sin and death. ROMANS 8:1–2

36) Marital Mismatch

Now the name of the man was Nabal; and the name of his wife Abigail: and she was a woman of good understanding, and of a beautiful countenance: but the man was churlish and evil in his doings; and he was of the house of Caleb. 1 SAMUEL 25:3

Then his father and his mother said unto him, Is there never a woman among the daughters of thy brethren, or among all my people, that thou goest to take a wife of the uncircumcised Philistines? And Samson said unto his father, Get her for me; for she pleaseth me well. JUDGES 14:3

37) Gospel Villain

Then entered Satan into Judas surnamed Iscariot, being of the number of the twelve. And he went his way, and communed with the chief priests and captains, how he might betray him unto them. LUKE 22:3–4

Saying, I have sinned in that I have betrayed the innocent blood. And they said, What is that to us? see thou to that. And he cast down the pieces of silver in the temple, and departed, and went and hanged himself. MATTHEW 27:4–5

38) Thoughts for Philemon

I Paul have written it with mine own hand, I will repay it: albeit I do not say to thee how thou owest unto me even thine own self besides. PHILEMON 19

I thank my God, making mention of thee always in my prayers, hearing of thy love and faith, which thou hast toward the Lord Jesus, and toward all saints; that the communication of thy faith may become effectual by the acknowledging of every good thing which is in you in Christ Jesus. PHILEMON 4–6

39) Goats in the Bible

Or if his sin, which he hath sinned, come to his knowledge: then he shall bring his offering, a kid of the goats, a female without blemish, for his sin which he hath sinned. LEVITICUS 4:28

Then Saul took three thousand chosen men out of all Israel, and went to seek David and his men upon the rocks of the wild goats. 1 SAMUEL 24:2

40) Days of Creation

And God said, Let there be lights in the firmament of the heaven to divide the day from the night; and let them be for signs, and for seasons, and for days, and years: And let them be for lights in the firmament of the heaven to give light upon the earth: and it was so. GENESIS 1:14–15

And God created great whales, and every living creature that moveth, which the waters brought forth abundantly, after their kind, and every winged fowl after his kind: and God saw that it was good. And God blessed them, saying, Be fruitful, and multiply. GENESIS 1:21–22

41) Cities in Acts

And a certain woman named Lydia, a seller of purple, of the city of Thyatira, which worshipped God, heard us: whose heart the Lord opened, that she attended unto the things which were spoken of Paul. ACTS 16:14

And the brethren immediately sent away Paul and Silas by night unto Berea: who coming thither went into the synagogue of the Jews. ACTS 17:10

42) Old Testament Mothers

Wherefore it came to pass, when the time was come about after Hannah had conceived, that she bare a son, and called his name Samuel, saying, Because I have asked him of the LORD. 1 SAMUEL 1:20

And Hagar bare Abram a son: and Abram called his son's name, which Hagar bare, Ishmael. GENESIS 16:15

43) More Old Testament Mothers

For Sarah conceived, and bare Abraham a son in his old age, at the set time of which God had spoken to him. GENESIS 21:2

So Boaz took Ruth, and she was his wife: and when he went in unto her, the LORD gave her conception, and she bare a son. RUTH 4:13

44) Jesus' Words to the Churches

So then because thou art lukewarm, and neither cold nor hot, I will spue thee out of my mouth. REVELATION 3:16

He that overcometh, the same shall be clothed in white raiment; and I will not blot out his name out of the book of life, but I will confess his name before my Father, and before his angels. REVELATION 3:5

45) Animals of the Bible

Every three years once came the ships of Tarshish bringing gold, and silver, ivory, and apes, and peacocks. 2 CHRONICLES 9:21

The wolf also shall dwell with the lamb, and the leopard shall lie down with the kid; and the calf and the young lion and the fatling together; and a little child shall lead them. ISAIAH 11:6

46) Miracles of Paul

And God wrought special miracles by the hands of Paul: So that from his body were brought unto the sick handkerchiefs or aprons, and the diseases departed from them, and the evil spirits went out of them. ACTS 19:11–12

And it came to pass, that the father of Publius lay sick of a fever and of a bloody flux: to whom Paul entered in, and prayed, and laid his hands on him, and healed him. ACTS 28:8

47) Proverbally Speaking, Part 1

When wisdom entereth into thine heart, and knowledge is pleasant unto thy soul; discretion shall preserve thee, understanding shall keep thee. PROVERBS 2:10–11

The blessing of the LORD, it maketh rich, and he addeth no sorrow with it. PROVERBS 10:22

48) Proverbally Speaking, Part 2

How much better is it to get wisdom than gold! and to get understanding rather to be chosen than silver! PROVERBS 16:16

Make no friendship with an angry man; and with a furious man thou shalt not go: Lest thou learn his ways, and get a snare to thy soul. PROVERBS 22:24–25

49) Ex-Queens

And the king loved Esther above all the women, and she obtained grace and favour in his sight more than all the virgins; so that he set the royal crown upon her head, and made her queen instead of Vashti. ESTHER 2:17

Wherefore they came again, and told him. And he said, This is the word of the LORD, which he spake by his servant Elijah the Tishbite, saying, In the portion of Jezreel shall dogs eat the flesh of Jezebel. 2 KINGS 9:36

50) A Note from Jude

Beloved, when I gave all diligence to write unto you of the common salvation, it was needful for me to write unto you, and exhort you that ye should earnestly contend for the faith which was once delivered unto the saints. JUDE 3

Now unto him that is able to keep you from falling, and to present you faultless before the presence of his glory with exceeding joy, to the only wise God our Saviour, be glory and majesty, dominion and power. JUDE 24–25

51) Ezekiel's Visions

The hand of the LORD was upon me, and carried me out in the spirit of the LORD, and set me down in the midst of the valley which was full of bones. EZEKIEL 37:1

And I looked, and, behold, a whirlwind came out of the north, a great cloud, and a fire infolding itself, and a brightness was about it, and out of the midst thereof as the colour of amber, out of the midst of the fire. Also out of the midst thereof came the likeness of four living creatures. And this was their appearance; they had the likeness of a man. EZEKIEL 1:4–5

52) On the Menu

And when the children of Israel saw it, they said one to another, It is manna: for they wist not what it was. And Moses said unto them, This is the bread which the LORD hath given you to eat. EXODUS 16:15

And John was clothed with camel's hair, and with a girdle of a skin about his loins; and he did eat locusts and wild honey. MARK 1:6

53) Off the Menu

Ye shall not eat of any thing that dieth of itself: thou shalt give it unto the stranger that is in thy gates, that he may eat it. DEUTERONOMY 14:21

And the swine, though he divide the hoof, and be clovenfooted, yet he cheweth not the cud; he is unclean to you. LEVITICUS 11:7

54) Modes of Transportation

Tell ye the daughter of Sion, Behold, thy King cometh unto thee, meek, and sitting upon an ass, and a colt the foal of an ass. MATTHEW 21:5

And Joseph made ready his chariot, and went up to meet Israel his father, to Goshen, and presented himself unto him; and he fell on his neck, and wept on his neck a good while. GENESIS 46:29

55) 2 Corinthians

While we look not at the things which are seen, but at the things which are not seen: for the things which are seen are temporal; but the things which are not seen are eternal. 2 CORINTHIANS 4:18

Examine yourselves, whether ye be in the faith; prove your own selves. Know ye not your own selves, how that Jesus Christ is in you, except ye be reprobates? 2 CORINTHIANS 13:5

56) The Number of Perfection

And God blessed the seventh day, and sanctified it: because that in it he had rested from all his work which God created and made. GENESIS 2:3

And there came unto me one of the seven angels which had the seven vials full of the seven last plagues, and talked with me, saying, Come hither, I will shew thee the bride, the Lamb's wife. REVELATION 21:9

57) Poor Job, Part 1

And the LORD said unto Satan, Hast thou considered my servant Job, that there is none like him in the earth, a perfect and an upright man, one that feareth God, and escheweth evil? JOB 1:8

Then Satan answered the LORD, and said, Doth Job fear God for nought? Hast not thou made an hedge about him, and about his house, and about all that he hath on every side? JOB 1:9–10

58) Poor Job, Part 2

So they sat down with him upon the ground seven days and seven nights, and none spake a word unto him: for they saw that his grief was very great. JOB 2:13

Then Job arose, and rent his mantle, and shaved his head, and fell down upon the ground, and worshipped, and said, Naked came I out of my mother's womb, and naked shall I return thither: the LORD gave, and the LORD hath taken away. JOB 1:20–21

59) Job Restored

Then Job answered the LORD, and said, I know that thou canst do every thing, and that no thought can be withholden from thee. JOB 42:1–2

So the LORD blessed the latter end of Job more than his beginning: for he had fourteen thousand sheep, and six thousand camels, and a thousand yoke of oxen, and a thousand she asses. He had also seven sons and three daughters. JOB 42:12–13

60) The Crucifixion

And when they were come to the place, which is called Calvary, there they crucified him, and the malefactors, one on the right hand, and the other on the left. LUKE 23:33

And after that they had mocked him, they took the robe off from him, and put his own raiment on him, and led him away to crucify him. And as they came out, they found a man of Cyrene, Simon by name: him they compelled to bear his cross. MATTHEW 27:31–32

61) Gideon

Behold, I will put a fleece of wool in the floor; and if the dew be on the fleece only, and it be dry upon all the earth beside, then shall I know that thou wilt save Israel by mine hand, as thou hast said. JUDGES 6:37

And the three companies blew the trumpets, and brake the pitchers, and held the lamps in their left hands, and the trumpets in their right hands to blow withal: and they cried, The sword of the LORD, and of Gideon. JUDGES 7:20

62) Temptation

There hath no temptation taken you but such as is common to man: but God is faithful, who will not suffer you to be tempted above that ye are able; but will with the temptation also make a way to escape, that ye may be able to bear it. 1 CORINTHIANS 10:13

Be sober, be vigilant; because your adversary the devil, as a roaring lion, walketh about, seeking whom he may devour: whom resist stedfast in the faith. 1 PETER 5:8–9

63) Framed

And Ahab came into his house heavy and displeased because of the word which Naboth the Jezreelite had spoken to him: for he had said, I will not give thee the inheritance of my fathers. . . . But Jezebel his wife came to him, and said unto him, Why is thy spirit so sad, that thou eatest no bread? 1 KINGS 21:4–5

Proclaim a fast, and set Naboth on high among the people: And set two men, sons of Belial, before him, to bear witness against him, saying, Thou didst blaspheme God and the king. And then carry him out, and stone him. 1 KINGS 21:9–10

64) Protecting Marriage

Drink waters out of thine own cistern, and running waters out of thine own well. PROVERBS 5:15

Let thy fountain be blessed: and rejoice with the wife of thy youth. Let her be as the loving hind and pleasant roe; let her breasts satisfy thee at all times; and be thou ravished always with her love. PROVERBS 5:18–19

65) From the Book of Galatians

Christ hath redeemed us from the curse of the law, being made a curse for us: for it is written, Cursed is every one that hangeth on a tree. GALATIANS 3:13

Knowing that a man is not justified by the works of the law, but by the faith of Jesus Christ, even we have believed in Jesus Christ, that we might be justified by the faith of Christ, and not by the works of the law: for by the works of the law shall no flesh be justified. GALATIANS 2:16

66) Snakes in the Bible

Therefore the people came to Moses, and said, We have sinned, for we have spoken against the LORD, and against thee; pray unto the LORD, that he take away the serpents from us. And Moses prayed for the people. NUMBERS 21:7

And when Paul had gathered a bundle of sticks, and laid them on the fire, there came a viper out of the heat, and fastened on his hand. ACTS 28:3

67) True Beauty

Who can find a virtuous woman? for her price is far above rubies. The heart of her husband doth safely trust in her, so that he shall have no need of spoil. PROVERBS 31:10–11

Whose adorning let it not be that outward adorning of plaiting the hair, and of wearing of gold, or of putting on of apparel; but let it be the hidden man of the heart, in that which is not corruptible, even the ornament of a meek and quiet spirit. 1 Peter 3:3–4

68) A Little R & R

The sleep of a labouring man is sweet, whether he eat little or much: but the abundance of the rich will not suffer him to sleep. Ecclesiastes 5:12

And he said unto them, Come ye yourselves apart into a desert place, and rest a while: for there were many coming and going, and they had no leisure so much as to eat. Mark 6:31

69) Quotable Exodus

I am the Lord thy God, which have brought thee out of the land of Egypt, out of the house of bondage. Thou shalt have no other gods before me. Exodus 20:2–3

And he said, I will make all my goodness pass before thee, and I will proclaim the name of the Lord before thee; and will be gracious to whom I will be gracious, and will shew mercy on whom I will shew mercy. Exodus 33:19

70) Friends of Jesus

Now Jesus loved Martha, and her sister, and Lazarus. When he had heard therefore that he was sick, he abode two days still in the same place where he was. John 11:5–6

One of the two which heard John speak, and followed him, was Andrew, Simon Peter's brother. He first findeth his own brother Simon, and saith unto him, We have found the Messias, which is, being interpreted, the Christ. John 1:40–41

71) Animal Miracles

And the Lord opened the mouth of the ass, and she said unto Balaam, What have I done unto thee, that thou hast smitten me these three times? Numbers 22:28

Notwithstanding, lest we should offend them, go thou to the sea, and cast an hook, and take up the fish that first cometh up; and when thou hast opened his mouth, thou shalt find a piece of money: that take, and give unto them for me and thee. Matthew 17:27

72) Secretaries

Then Jeremiah called Baruch the son of Neriah: and Baruch wrote from the mouth of Jeremiah all the words of the Lord, which he had spoken unto him, upon a roll of a book. Jeremiah 36:4

I Tertius, who wrote this epistle, salute you in the Lord. Romans 16:22

73) The Night Sky

Which maketh Arcturus, Orion, and Pleiades, and the chambers of the south. Which doeth great things past finding out; yea, and wonders without number. Job 9:9–10

Therefore sprang there even of one, and him as good as dead, so many as the stars of the sky in multitude, and as the sand which is by the sea shore innumerable. Hebrews 11:12

74) First Christmas

Now all this was done, that it might be fulfilled which was spoken of the Lord by the prophet, saying, Behold, a virgin shall be with child, and shall bring forth a son, and they shall call his name Emmanuel. Matthew 1:22–23

And so it was, that, while they were there, the days were accomplished that she should be delivered. And she brought forth her firstborn son, and wrapped him in swaddling clothes, and laid him in a manger; because there was no room for them in the inn. Luke 2:6–7

75) Shadrach, Meshach, and Abednego

If it be so, our God whom we serve

is able to deliver us from the burning fiery furnace, and he will deliver us out of thine hand, O king. But if not, be it known unto thee, O king, that we will not serve thy gods, nor worship the golden image which thou hast set up. Daniel 3:17–18

And the princes, governors, and captains, and the king's counsellors, being gathered together, saw these men, upon whose bodies the fire had no power, nor was an hair of their head singed, neither were their coats changed, nor the smell of fire had passed on them. Daniel 3:27

76) Mysterious Creatures

Behold now behemoth, which I made with thee; he eateth grass as an ox. Job 40:15

In that day the Lord with his sore and great and strong sword shall punish leviathan the piercing serpent, even leviathan that crooked serpent; and he shall slay the dragon that is in the sea. Isaiah 27:1

77) The Fall of Jericho

And they utterly destroyed all that was in the city, both man and woman, young and old, and ox, and sheep, and ass, with the edge of the sword. Joshua 6:21

And it shall come to pass, that when they make a long blast with the ram's horn, and when ye hear the sound of the trumpet, all the people shall shout with a great shout; and the wall of the city shall fall down flat, and the people shall ascend up every man straight before him. Joshua 6:5

78) Hosea

Then said the Lord unto me, Go yet, love a woman beloved of her friend, yet an adulteress, according to the love of the Lord toward the children of Israel, who look to other gods, and love flagons of wine. Hosea 3:1

I will heal their backsliding, I will love them freely: for mine anger is turned away from him. I will be as the dew unto Israel: he shall grow as the lily, and cast forth his roots as Lebanon. HOSEA 14:4–5

79) Money, Money, Money

And Abraham hearkened unto Ephron; and Abraham weighed to Ephron the silver, which he had named in the audience of the sons of Heth, four hundred shekels of silver, current money with the merchant. GENESIS 23:16

And Jesus sat over against the treasury, and beheld how the people cast money into the treasury: and many that were rich cast in much. And there came a certain poor widow, and she threw in two mites, which make a farthing. MARK 12:41–42

80) Get Saved!

For with the heart man believeth unto righteousness; and with the mouth confession is made unto salvation. ROMANS 10:10

Wherefore, my beloved, as ye have always obeyed, not as in my presence only, but now much more in my absence, work out your own salvation with fear and trembling. PHILIPPIANS 2:12

81) Letter to Thessalonica

Now God himself and our Father, and our Lord Jesus Christ, direct our way unto you. And the Lord make you to increase and abound in love one toward another, and toward all men, even as we do toward you. 1 THESSALONIANS 3:11–12

Now we exhort you, brethren, warn them that are unruly, comfort the feebleminded, support the weak, be patient toward all men. See that none render evil for evil unto any man; but ever follow that which is good, both among yourselves, and to all men. 1 THESSALONIANS 5:14–15

82) Familiar Phrases

Keep me as the apple of the eye, hide me under the shadow of thy wings. PSALM 17:8

Thy watchmen shall lift up the voice; with the voice together shall they sing: for they shall see eye to eye, when the LORD shall bring again Zion. ISAIAH 52:8

83) More Familiar Phrases

Who is he that will plead with me? for now, if I hold my tongue, I shall give up the ghost. JOB 13:19

To the weak became I as weak, that I might gain the weak: I am made all things to all men, that I might by all means save some. 1 CORINTHIANS 9:22

84) You Swine!

And he said unto them, Go. And when they were come out, they went into the herd of swine: and, behold, the whole herd of swine ran violently down a steep place into the sea, and perished in the waters. MATTHEW 8:32

As a jewel of gold in a swine's snout, so is a fair woman which is without discretion. PROVERBS 11:22

85) Mounts and Mountains

And the ark rested in the seventh month, on the seventeenth day of the month, upon the mountains of Ararat. And the waters decreased continually until the tenth month: in the tenth month, on the first day of the month, were the tops of the mountains seen. GENESIS 8:4–5

Gather to me all Israel unto mount Carmel, and the prophets of Baal four hundred and fifty, and the prophets of the groves four hundred, which eat at Jezebel's table. So Ahab sent unto all the children of Israel, and gathered the prophets. 1 KINGS 18:19–20

86) Bible Occupations

Send therefore to Joppa, and call hither Simon, whose surname is Peter; he is lodged in the house of one Simon a tanner by the sea side: who, when he cometh, shall speak unto thee. ACTS 10:32

When Jesus heard it, he saith unto them, They that are whole have no need of the physician, but they that are sick: I came not to call the righteous, but sinners to repentance. MARK 2:17

87) More Bible Occupations

Then answered Amos, and said to Amaziah, I was no prophet, neither was I a prophet's son; but I was an herdman, and a gatherer of sycomore fruit. AMOS 7:14

Demetrius, a silversmith, which made silver shrines for Diana, brought no small gain unto the craftsmen; whom he called together with the workmen of like occupation, and said, Sirs, ye know that by this craft we have our wealth. ACTS 19:24–25

88) Even More Bible Occupations

Be ye ashamed, O ye husbandmen; howl, O ye vinedressers, for the wheat and for the barley; because the harvest of the field is perished. JOEL 1:11

And Jesus said unto the centurion, Go thy way; and as thou hast believed, so be it done unto thee. And his servant was healed in the selfsame hour. MATTHEW 8:13

89) Theological Terms

Therefore as by the offence of one judgment came upon all men to condemnation; even so by the righteousness of one the free gift came upon all men unto justification of life. ROMANS 5:18

Elect according to the foreknowledge of God the Father, through sanctification of the Spirit, unto obedience and sprinkling of the blood of Jesus Christ: Grace unto you, and peace, be multiplied. 1 Peter 1:2

90) Strong Women

Then Jael Heber's wife took a nail of the tent, and took an hammer in her hand, and went softly unto him, and smote the nail into his temples, and fastened it into the ground: for he was fast asleep and weary. So he died. Judges 4:21

And Deborah, a prophetess, the wife of Lapidoth, she judged Israel at that time. And she dwelt under the palm tree of Deborah between Ramah and Bethel in mount Ephraim: and the children of Israel came up to her for judgment. Judges 4:4–5

91) Nehemiah's Story, Part 1

And I said unto the king, If it please the king, and if thy servant have found favour in thy sight, that thou wouldest send me unto Judah, unto the city of my fathers' sepulchres, that I may build it. Nehemiah 2:5

O Lord, I beseech thee, let now thine ear be attentive to the prayer of thy servant, and to the prayer of thy servants, who desire to fear thy name: and prosper, I pray thee, thy servant this day, and grant him mercy in the sight of this man. For I was the king's cupbearer. Nehemiah 1:11

92) Nehemiah's Story, Part 2

They which builded on the wall, and they that bare burdens, with those that laded, every one with one of his hands wrought in the work, and with the other hand held a weapon. Nehemiah 4:17

So the wall was finished. . . . And it came to pass, that when all our enemies heard thereof, and all the heathen that were about us saw these things, they were much cast down in their own eyes: for they perceived that this work was wrought of our God. Nehemiah 6:15–16

93) Repent!

From that time Jesus began to preach, and to say, Repent: for the kingdom of heaven is at hand. Matthew 4:17

As I live, saith the Lord God, I have no pleasure in the death of the wicked; but that the wicked turn from his way and live. Ezekiel 33:11

94) Named Angels

And there was war in heaven: Michael and his angels fought against the dragon; and the dragon fought and his angels. Revelation 12:7

And the angel answering said unto him, I am Gabriel, that stand in the presence of God; and am sent to speak unto thee, and to shew thee these glad tidings. Luke 1:19

95) Big Cats

And so it was at the beginning of their dwelling there, that they feared not the Lord: therefore the Lord sent lions among them, which slew some of them. 2 Kings 17:25

And when the prophet that brought him back from the way heard thereof, he said, It is the man of God, who was disobedient unto the word of the Lord: therefore the Lord hath delivered him unto the lion, which hath torn him, and slain him. 1 Kings 13:26

96) Scripture on Scripture

For the word of God is quick, and powerful, and sharper than any twoedged sword, piercing even to the dividing asunder of soul and spirit, and of the joints and marrow, and is a discerner of the thoughts and intents of the heart. Hebrews 4:12

Knowing this first, that no prophecy of the scripture is of any private interpretation. For the prophecy came not in old time by the will of man: but holy men of God spake as they were moved by the Holy Ghost. 2 Peter 1:20–21

97) Off to School

Wherefore the law was our schoolmaster to bring us unto Christ, that we might be justified by faith. But after that faith is come, we are no longer under a schoolmaster. Galatians 3:24–25

But when divers were hardened, and believed not, but spake evil of that way before the multitude, he departed from them, and separated the disciples, disputing daily in the school of one Tyrannus. Acts 19:9

98) Elect Me!

(For the children being not yet born, neither having done any good or evil, that the purpose of God according to election might stand, not of works, but of him that calleth.) Romans 9:11

Wherefore the rather, brethren, give diligence to make your calling and election sure: for if ye do these things, ye shall never fall: For so an entrance shall be ministered unto you abundantly into the everlasting kingdom of our Lord and Saviour Jesus Christ. 2 Peter 1:10–11

99) Tools in the Bible

And on all hills that shall be digged with the mattock, there shall not come thither the fear of briers and thorns: but it shall be for the sending forth of oxen, and for the treading of lesser cattle. Isaiah 7:25

And the house, when it was in building, was built of stone made ready before it was brought thither: so that there was neither hammer nor axe nor any tool of iron heard in the house, while it was in building. 1 Kings 6:7

100) The Life of Peter

And when Peter was come down out of the ship, he walked on the water, to go to Jesus. MATTHEW 14:29

Then Peter said, Silver and gold have I none; but such as I have give I thee: In the name of Jesus Christ of Nazareth rise up and walk. ACTS 3:6

101) God's People

If my people, which are called by my name, shall humble themselves, and pray, and seek my face, and turn from their wicked ways; then will I hear from heaven, and will forgive their sin, and will heal their land. 2 CHRONICLES 7:14

But ye are a chosen generation, a royal priesthood, an holy nation, a peculiar people. 1 PETER 2:9

102) Sacrifices

And Abraham took the wood of the burnt offering, and laid it upon Isaac his son; and he took the fire in his hand, and a knife; and they went both of them together. GENESIS 22:6

By the which will we are sanctified through the offering of the body of Jesus Christ once for all. HEBREWS 10:10

103) Not Man's Best Friend

And of Jezebel also spake the LORD, saying, The dogs shall eat Jezebel by the wall of Jezreel. 1 KINGS 21:23

For dogs have compassed me: the assembly of the wicked have inclosed me: they pierced my hands and my feet. PSALM 22:16

104) The Awesomeness of God, Part 1

Who is the blessed and only Potentate, the King of kings, and Lord of lords; who only hath immortality, dwelling in the light which no man can approach unto; whom no man hath seen, nor can see: to whom be honour and power

everlasting. 1 TIMOTHY 6:15–16

For thus saith the high and lofty One that inhabiteth eternity, whose name is Holy; I dwell in the high and holy place, with him also that is of a contrite and humble spirit. ISAIAH 57:15

105) The Awesomeness of God, Part 2

Then said I, Woe is me! for I am undone; because I am a man of unclean lips, and I dwell in the midst of a people of unclean lips: for mine eyes have seen the King, the LORD of hosts. ISAIAH 6:5

I am Alpha and Omega, the beginning and the ending, saith the Lord, which is, and which was, and which is to come, the Almighty. REVELATION 1:8

106) Scenes by the River

If they will not believe also these two signs, neither hearken unto thy voice, that thou shalt take of the water of the river, and pour it upon the dry land: and the water which thou takest out of the river shall become blood upon the dry land. EXODUS 4:9

Rabbi, he that was with thee beyond Jordan, to whom thou barest witness, behold, the same baptizeth, and all men come to him. John answered and said, A man can receive nothing, except it be given him from heaven. JOHN 3:26–27

107) An Even Dozen

All these are the twelve tribes of Israel: and this is it that their father spake unto them, and blessed them; every one. GENESIS 49:28

And it came to pass afterward, that he went throughout every city and village, preaching and shewing the glad tidings of the kingdom of God: and the twelve were with him. LUKE 8:1

108) The Story of Zacchaeus

And he sought to see Jesus who he was; and could not for the press, because he was little of stature. And he ran before, and climbed up into a sycomore tree to see him: for he was to pass that way. LUKE 19:3–4

And Jesus said unto him, This day is salvation come to this house, forsomuch as he also is a son of Abraham. For the Son of man is come to seek and to save that which was lost. LUKE 19:9–10

109) Moses' Sister

And the cloud departed from off the tabernacle; and, behold, Miriam became leprous, white as snow: and Aaron looked upon Miriam, and, behold, she was leprous. NUMBERS 12:10

And Miriam the prophetess, the sister of Aaron, took a timbrel in her hand; and all the women went out after her with timbrels and with dances. And Miriam answered them, Sing ye to the LORD, for he hath triumphed gloriously. EXODUS 15:20–21

110) Cows in the Bible

And God made the beast of the earth after his kind, and cattle after their kind, and every thing that creepeth upon the earth after his kind: and God saw that it was good. GENESIS 1:25

And the LORD shall make thee plenteous in goods, in the fruit of thy body, and in the fruit of thy cattle, and in the fruit of thy ground, in the land which the LORD sware unto thy fathers to give thee. DEUTERONOMY 28:11

111) Holy, Holy, Holy

O God, thou art terrible out of thy holy places: the God of Israel is he that giveth strength and power unto his people. Blessed be God. PSALM 68:35

And when the LORD saw that he turned

aside to see, God called unto him out of the midst of the bush, and said, Moses, Moses. And he said, Here am I. And he said, Draw not nigh hither: put off thy shoes from off thy feet, for the place whereon thou standest is holy ground. EXODUS 3:4–5

112) Makin' Music

Speaking to yourselves in psalms and hymns and spiritual songs, singing and making melody in your heart to the Lord; giving thanks always for all things unto God. EPHESIANS 5:19–20

As the trumpeters and singers were as one, to make one sound to be heard in praising and thanking the LORD; and when they lifted up their voice with the trumpets and cymbals and instruments of musick, and praised the LORD, saying, For he is good; for his mercy endureth for ever: that then the house was filled with a cloud. 2 CHRONICLES 5:13

113) Bones

And Moses took the bones of Joseph with him: for he had straitly sworn the children of Israel, saying, God will surely visit you; and ye shall carry up my bones away hence with you. EXODUS 13:19

They arose, all the valiant men, and took away the body of Saul, and the bodies of his sons, and brought them to Jabesh, and buried their bones under the oak in Jabesh, and fasted seven days. 1 CHRONICLES 10:12

114) From Psalm 119

With my lips have I declared all the judgments of thy mouth. I have rejoiced in the way of thy testimonies, as much as in all riches. I will meditate in thy precepts, and have respect unto thy ways. PSALM 119:13–15

Give me understanding, and I shall keep thy law; yea, I shall observe it with my whole heart. Make me to go in the path of thy commandments; for therein do I delight. PSALM 119:34–35

115) More from Psalm 119

The earth, O LORD, is full of thy mercy: teach me thy statutes. Thou hast dealt well with thy servant, O LORD, according unto thy word. Teach me good judgment and knowledge: for I have believed thy commandments. PSALM 119:64–66

The wicked have laid a snare for me: yet I erred not from thy precepts. Thy testimonies have I taken as an heritage for ever: for they are the rejoicing of my heart. I have inclined mine heart to perform thy statutes alway, even unto the end. PSALM 119:110–112

116) Giant Trouble

And there went out a champion out of the camp of the Philistines, named Goliath, of Gath, whose height was six cubits and a span. 1 SAMUEL 17:4

And yet again there was war at Gath, where was a man of great stature, whose fingers and toes were four and twenty, six on each hand, and six on each foot and he also was the son of the giant. 1 CHRONICLES 20:6

117) New Testament Rulers

Now when Jesus was born in Bethlehem of Judaea in the days of Herod the king, behold, there came wise men from the east to Jerusalem. MATTHEW 2:1

And Jesus answering said unto them, Render to Caesar the things that are Caesar's, and to God the things that are God's. MARK 12:17

118) A Babylonian King

Then Nebuchadnezzar the king sent to gather together the princes, the governors, and the captains, the judges, the treasurers, the counsellors, the sheriffs, and all the rulers of the provinces, to come to the dedication of the image which Nebuchadnezzar the king had set up. DANIEL 3:2

Then Nebuchadnezzar spake, and said, Blessed be the God of Shadrach, Meshach, and Abednego, who hath sent his angel, and delivered his servants that trusted in him, and have changed the king's word. DANIEL 3:28

119) Rules for Church Leaders

A bishop then must be blameless, the husband of one wife, vigilant, sober, of good behaviour, given to hospitality, apt to teach; not given to wine, no striker, not greedy of filthy lucre; but patient, not a brawler, not covetous. 1 TIMOTHY 3:2–3

Then the twelve called the multitude of the disciples unto them, and said, It is not reason that we should leave the word of God, and serve tables. Wherefore, brethren, look ye out among you seven men of honest report, full of the Holy Ghost and wisdom. ACTS 6:2–3

120) Spiritual U-Turns

Say unto them, As I live, saith the Lord GOD, I have no pleasure in the death of the wicked; but that the wicked turn from his way and live: turn ye, turn ye from your evil ways; for why will ye die, O house of Israel? EZEKIEL 33:11

Turn, O backsliding children, saith the LORD; for I am married unto you: and I will take you one of a city, and two of a family, and I will bring you to Zion. JEREMIAH 3:14

121) Hellish Stuff

And if thy hand offend thee, cut it off: it is better for thee to enter into life maimed, than having two hands to go into hell, into the fire that never shall be quenched: where their worm dieth not, and the fire is not quenched. MARK 9:43–44

And the beast was taken, and with him

the false prophet that wrought miracles before him, with which he deceived them that had received the mark of the beast, and them that worshipped his image. These both were cast alive into a lake of fire burning with brimstone. Revelation 19:20

122) More Hellish Stuff

But the fearful, and unbelieving, and the abominable, and murderers, and whoremongers, and sorcerers, and idolaters, and all liars, shall have their part in the lake which burneth with fire and brimstone: which is the second death. Revelation 21:8

Send Lazarus, that he may dip the tip of his finger in water, and cool my tongue; for I am tormented in this flame. But Abraham said, Son, remember that thou in thy lifetime receivedst thy good things, and likewise Lazarus evil things: but now he is comforted, and thou art tormented. Luke 16:24–25

123) Heavenly Stuff

And he said unto Jesus, Lord, remember me when thou comest into thy kingdom. And Jesus said unto him, Verily I say unto thee, Today shalt thou be with me in paradise. Luke 23:42–43

And I knew such a man, (whether in the body, or out of the body, I cannot tell: God knoweth;) how that he was caught up into paradise, and heard unspeakable words, which it is not lawful for a man to utter. 2 Corinthians 12:3–4

124) More Heavenly Stuff

Him that overcometh will I make a pillar in the temple of my God, and he shall go no more out: and I will write upon him the name of my God, and the name of the city of my God, which is new Jerusalem, which cometh down out of heaven from my God: and I will write upon him my new name. Revelation 3:12

Now when all the people were baptized, it came to pass, that Jesus also being baptized, and praying, the heaven was opened, and the Holy Ghost descended in a bodily shape like a dove upon him, and a voice came from heaven, which said, Thou art my beloved Son. Luke 3:21–22

125) Lesser-Known Disciples

Judas saith unto him, not Iscariot, Lord, how is it that thou wilt manifest thyself unto us, and not unto the world? John 14:22

We have found him, of whom Moses in the law, and the prophets, did write, Jesus of Nazareth, the son of Joseph. And Nathanael said unto him, Can there any good thing come out of Nazareth? Philip saith unto him, Come and see. John 1:45–46

126) Biblical Horses

For the horse of Pharaoh went in with his chariots and with his horsemen into the sea, and the Lord brought again the waters of the sea upon them; but the children of Israel went on dry land in the midst of the sea. Exodus 15:19

And number thee an army, like the army that thou hast lost, horse for horse, and chariot for chariot: and we will fight against them in the plain, and surely we shall be stronger than they. And he hearkened unto their voice, and did so. 1 Kings 20:25

127) Villains

Alexander the coppersmith did me much evil: the Lord reward him according to his works: of whom be thou ware also; for he hath greatly withstood our words. 2 Timothy 4:14–15

And he thought scorn to lay hands on Mordecai alone; for they had shewed him the people of Mordecai: wherefore Haman sought to destroy all the Jews

that were throughout the whole kingdom of Ahasuerus, even the people of Mordecai. Esther 3:6

128) Noah's Ark

And this is the fashion which thou shalt make it of: The length of the ark shall be three hundred cubits, the breadth of it fifty cubits, and the height of it thirty cubits. Genesis 6:15

There went in two and two unto Noah into the ark, the male and the female, as God had commanded Noah. Genesis 7:9

129) Executions

And she, being before instructed of her mother, said, Give me here John Baptist's head in a charger. Matthew 14:8

So they hanged Haman on the gallows that he had prepared for Mordecai. Then was the king's wrath pacified. Esther 7:10

130) Fish Fry

These ye shall eat of all that are in the waters: all that have fins and scales shall ye eat. Deuteronomy 14:9

As soon then as they were come to land, they saw a fire of coals there, and fish laid thereon, and bread. John 21:9

131) Planting and Harvesting

They have sown wheat, but shall reap thorns: they have put themselves to pain, but shall not profit: and they shall be ashamed of your revenues because of the fierce anger of the Lord. Jeremiah 12:13

Be not deceived; God is not mocked: for whatsoever a man soweth, that shall he also reap. For he that soweth to his flesh shall of the flesh reap corruption; but he that soweth to the Spirit shall of the Spirit reap life everlasting. Galatians 6:7–8

132) Other Farm Analogies

Whose fan is in his hand, and he will throughly purge his floor, and gather his wheat into the garner; but he will burn up the chaff with unquenchable fire. MATTHEW 3:12

Put ye in the sickle, for the harvest is ripe: come, get you down; for the press is full, the fats overflow; for their wickedness is great. JOEL 3:13

133) Athletics in the Bible

I therefore so run, not as uncertainly; so fight I, not as one that beateth the air: But I keep under my body, and bring it into subjection: lest that by any means, when I have preached to others, I myself should be a castaway. 1 CORINTHIANS 9:26–27

Wherefore seeing we also are compassed about with so great a cloud of witnesses, let us lay aside every weight, and the sin which doth so easily beset us, and let us run with patience the race that is set before us. HEBREWS 12:1

134) Weaponry

And the LORD said unto Joshua, Stretch out the spear that is in thy hand toward Ai; for I will give it into thine hand. And Joshua stretched out the spear that he had in his hand toward the city. JOSHUA 8:18

Whose arrows are sharp, and all their bows bent, their horses' hoofs shall be counted like flint, and their wheels like a whirlwind. ISAIAH 5:28

135) How Big Is God?

Am I a God at hand, saith the LORD, and not a God afar off? Can any hide himself in secret places that I shall not see him? saith the LORD. Do not I fill heaven and earth? saith the LORD. JEREMIAH 23:23–24

Whither shall I go from thy spirit? or whither shall I flee from thy presence? If I ascend up into heaven, thou art there: if I make my bed in hell, behold, thou art there. PSALM 139:7–8

136) Biblical Kisses

Mercy and truth are met together; righteousness and peace have kissed each other. PSALM 85:10

When Jacob saw Rachel the daughter of Laban his mother's brother, and the sheep of Laban his mother's brother, that Jacob went near, and rolled the stone from the well's mouth, and watered the flock of Laban his mother's brother. And Jacob kissed Rachel. GENESIS 29:10–11

137) Honesty Is the Best Policy

A false balance is abomination to the LORD: but a just weight is his delight. PROVERBS 11:1

And that ye put on the new man, which after God is created in righteousness and true holiness. Wherefore putting away lying, speak every man truth with his neighbour: for we are members one of another. EPHESIANS 4:24–25

138) Battle Scenes

And the LORD delivered it also, and the king thereof, into the hand of Israel; and he smote it with the edge of the sword, and all the souls that were therein; he let none remain in it; but did unto the king thereof as he did unto the king of Jericho. JOSHUA 10:30

The kings came and fought, then fought the kings of Canaan in Taanach by the waters of Megiddo; they took no gain of money. They fought from heaven; the stars in their courses fought against Sisera. JUDGES 5:19–20

139) Ancient Places

And he said unto him, I am the LORD that brought thee out of Ur of the Chaldees, to give thee this land to inherit it. GENESIS 15:7

There was a man in the land of Uz, whose name was Job; and that man was perfect and upright, and one that feared God, and eschewed evil. JOB 1:1

140) Crazy, Man

And David laid up these words in his heart, and was sore afraid of Achish the king of Gath. And he changed his behaviour before them, and feigned himself mad in their hands, and scrabbled on the doors of the gate, and let his spittle fall down upon his beard. 1 SAMUEL 21:12–13

Festus said with a loud voice, Paul, thou art beside thyself; much learning doth make thee mad. But he said, I am not mad, most noble Festus; but speak forth the words of truth and soberness. ACTS 26:24–25

141) Children of the Bible

And now, little children, abide in him; that, when he shall appear, we may have confidence, and not be ashamed before him at his coming. 1 JOHN 2:28

Then were there brought unto him little children, that he should put his hands on them, and pray: and the disciples rebuked them. But Jesus said, Suffer little children, and forbid them not, to come unto me: for of such is the kingdom of heaven. MATTHEW 19:13–14

142) It's Magic

There shall not be found among you any one that maketh his son or his daughter to pass through the fire, or that useth divination, or an observer of times, or an enchanter, or a witch. DEUTERONOMY 18:10

A man also or woman that hath a familiar spirit, or that is a wizard, shall surely be put to death: they shall stone them with stones: their blood shall be upon them. LEVITICUS 20:27

143) Craftsmanship

Cursed be the man that maketh any graven or molten image, an abomination unto the LORD, the work of the hands of the craftsman, and putteth it in a secret place. And all the people shall answer and say, Amen. DEUTERONOMY 27:15

And the voice of harpers, and musicians, and of pipers, and trumpeters, shall be heard no more at all in thee; and no craftsman, of whatsoever craft he be, shall be found any more in thee; and the sound of a millstone shall be heard no more at all in thee. REVELATION 18:22

144) God's Love

For when we were yet without strength, in due time Christ died for the ungodly. ROMANS 5:6

For I am persuaded, that neither death, nor life, nor angels, nor principalities, nor powers, nor things present, nor things to come, nor height, nor depth, nor any other creature, shall be able to separate us from the love of God, which is in Christ Jesus our Lord. ROMANS 8:38–39

145) On the Vine

Abide in me, and I in you. As the branch cannot bear fruit of itself, except it abide in the vine; no more can ye, except ye abide in me. JOHN 15:4

(For the fruit of the Spirit is in all goodness and righteousness and truth;) proving what is acceptable unto the Lord. EPHESIANS 5:9–10

146) Jesus Describes Himself

Then spake Jesus again unto them, saying, I am the light of the world: he that followeth me shall not walk in darkness, but shall have the light of life. JOHN 8:12

I am the door: by me if any man enter in, he shall be saved, and shall go in and out, and find pasture. The thief cometh not, but for to steal, and to kill, and to destroy: I am come that they might have life, and that they might have it more abundantly. JOHN 10:9–10

147) Paul Describes Himself

He cried out in the council, Men and brethren, I am a Pharisee, the son of a Pharisee: of the hope and resurrection of the dead I am called in question. ACTS 23:6

Circumcised the eighth day, of the stock of Israel, of the tribe of Benjamin, an Hebrew of the Hebrews; as touching the law, a Pharisee; concerning zeal, persecuting the church; touching the righteousness which is in the law, blameless. PHILIPPIANS 3:5–6

148) I'm Depressed

And it came to pass, when the sun did arise, that God prepared a vehement east wind; and the sun beat upon the head of Jonah, that he fainted, and wished in himself to die, and said, It is better for me to die than to live. JONAH 4:8

But he himself went a day's journey into the wilderness, and came and sat down under a juniper tree: and he requested for himself that he might die; and said, It is enough; now, O LORD, take away my life; for I am not better than my fathers. 1 KINGS 19:4

149) I'm Full of Joy

I will bless the LORD at all times: his praise shall continually be in my mouth. My soul shall make her boast in the LORD: the humble shall hear thereof, and be glad. PSALM 34:1–2

And Mary said, My soul doth magnify the Lord, and my spirit hath rejoiced in God my Saviour. For he hath regarded the low estate of his handmaiden: for, behold, from henceforth all generations shall call me blessed. LUKE 1:46–48

150) Solar Occurrences

And the sun stood still, and the moon stayed, until the people had avenged themselves upon their enemies. Is not this written in the book of Jasher? So the sun stood still in the midst of heaven. JOSHUA 10:13

And it was about the sixth hour, and there was a darkness over all the earth until the ninth hour. And the sun was darkened, and the veil of the temple was rent in the midst. And when Jesus had cried with a loud voice, he said, Father, into thy hands I commend my spirit. LUKE 23:44–46

151) Let's Party

And when these days were expired, the king made a feast unto all the people that were present in Shushan the palace, both unto great and small, seven days, in the court of the garden of the king's palace. ESTHER 1:5

When thou makest a dinner or a supper, call not thy friends, nor thy brethren, neither thy kinsmen, nor thy rich neighbours; lest they also bid thee again, and a recompence be made thee. But when thou makest a feast, call the poor, the maimed, the lame, the blind: and thou shalt be blessed. LUKE 14:12–14

152) Protected

The night is far spent, the day is at hand: let us therefore cast off the works of darkness, and let us put on the armour of light. ROMANS 13:12

Put on the whole armour of God, that ye may be able to stand against the wiles of the devil. For we wrestle not against flesh and blood, but against principalities, against powers, against the rulers of the darkness of this world, against spiritual wickedness in high places. EPHESIANS 6:11–12

153) Famous Names

By faith Abraham, when he was called to go out into a place which he should after receive for an inheritance, obeyed; and he went out, not knowing whither he went. HEBREWS 11:8

Then went king David in, and sat before the LORD, and he said, Who am I, O Lord GOD? and what is my house, that thou hast brought me hitherto? 2 SAMUEL 7:18

154) More Famous Names

And king Solomon shall be blessed, and the throne of David shall be established before the LORD for ever. 1 KINGS 2:45

Then Jonathan and David made a covenant, because he loved him as his own soul. 1 SAMUEL 18:3

155) The Temptation of Christ

And Jesus being full of the Holy Ghost returned from Jordan, and was led by the Spirit into the wilderness, being forty days tempted of the devil. And in those days he did eat nothing. LUKE 4:1–2

All this power will I give thee, and the glory of them: for that is delivered unto me; and to whomsoever I will give it. If thou therefore wilt worship me, all shall be thine. And Jesus answered and said unto him, Get thee behind me, Satan: for it is written, Thou shalt worship the Lord thy God. LUKE 4:6–8

156) The Avenger

To me belongeth vengeance and recompence; their foot shall slide in due time: for the day of their calamity is at hand, and the things that shall come upon them make haste. DEUTERONOMY 32:35

Say to them that are of a fearful heart, Be strong, fear not: behold, your God will come with vengeance, even God with a recompence; he will come and save you. ISAIAH 35:4

157) Valuables

But lay up for yourselves treasures in heaven, where neither moth nor rust doth corrupt, and where thieves do not break through nor steal: For where your treasure is, there will your heart be also. MATTHEW 6:20–21

But God said unto him, Thou fool, this night thy soul shall be required of thee: then whose shall those things be, which thou hast provided? So is he that layeth up treasure for himself, and is not rich toward God. LUKE 12:20–21

158) Dazed and Confused

And they were all amazed, insomuch that they questioned among themselves, saying, What thing is this? what new doctrine is this? for with authority commandeth he even the unclean spirits, and they do obey him. MARK 1:27

The multitude came together, and were confounded, because that every man heard them speak in his own language. And they were all amazed and marvelled, saying one to another, Behold, are not all these which speak Galilaeans? And how hear we every man in our own tongue? ACTS 2:6–8

159) The Shepherd

But when he saw the multitudes, he was moved with compassion on them, because they fainted, and were scattered abroad, as sheep having no shepherd. MATTHEW 9:36

I am the good shepherd, and know my sheep, and am known of mine. As the Father knoweth me, even so know I the Father: and I lay down my life for the sheep. JOHN 10:14–15

160) Fruit of the Vine

Do not drink wine nor strong drink, thou, nor thy sons with thee, when ye go into the tabernacle of the congre-gation, lest ye die: it shall be a statute for ever throughout your generations. LEVITICUS 10:9

Restore, I pray you, to them, even this day, their lands, their vineyards, their oliveyards, and their houses, also the hundredth part of the money, and of the corn, the wine, and the oil, that ye exact of them. NEHEMIAH 5:11

161) Love Songs

As the apple tree among the trees of the wood, so is my beloved among the sons. I sat down under his shadow with great delight, and his fruit was sweet to my taste. SONG OF SOLOMON 2:3

How fair is thy love, my sister, my spouse! how much better is thy love than wine! and the smell of thine ointments than all spices! SONG OF SOLOMON 4:10

162) Introducing Peter's Brother

And Jesus, walking by the sea of Galilee, saw two brethren, Simon called Peter, and Andrew his brother, casting a net into the sea: for they were fishers. MATTHEW 4:18

One of his disciples, Andrew, Simon Peter's brother, saith unto him, There is a lad here, which hath five barley loaves, and two small fishes: but what are they among so many? JOHN 6:8–9

163) Mysteries

There be three things which are too wonderful for me, yea, four which I know not: the way of an eagle in the air; the way of a serpent upon a rock; the way of a ship in the midst of the sea; and the way of a man with a maid. PROVERBS 30:18–19

Behold, I shew you a mystery; We shall not all sleep, but we shall all be changed, in a moment, in the twinkling of an eye, at the last trump: for the trumpet shall sound, and the dead shall be raised

incorruptible, and we shall be changed.
1 CORINTHIANS 15:51–52

164) Victory!

These shall make war with the Lamb, and the Lamb shall overcome them: for he is Lord of lords, and King of kings: And they that are with him are called, and chosen, and faithful.
REVELATION 17:14

These things I have spoken unto you, that in me ye might have peace. In the world ye shall have tribulation: but be of good cheer; I have overcome the world. JOHN 16:33

165) The Patriarchs, Part 1

Neither shall thy name any more be called Abram, but thy name shall be Abraham; for a father of many nations have I made thee. GENESIS 17:5

I am the God of Abraham thy father: fear not, for I am with thee, and will bless thee, and multiply thy seed for my servant Abraham's sake. And he builded an altar there, and called upon the name of the LORD, and pitched his tent there. GENESIS 26:24–25

166) The Patriarchs, Part 2

Behold, I have set the land before you: go in and possess the land which the LORD sware unto your fathers, Abraham, Isaac, and Jacob, to give unto them and to their seed after them.
DEUTERONOMY 1:8

And Jacob vowed a vow, saying, If God will be with me, and will keep me in this way that I go, and will give me bread to eat, and raiment to put on, so that I come again to my father's house in peace; then shall the LORD be my God. GENESIS 28:20–21

167) Stormy Weather

And, behold, there came a great wind from the wilderness, and smote the four corners of the house, and it fell upon

the young men, and they are dead; and I only am escaped alone to tell thee.
JOB 1:19

Behold, the LORD passed by, and a great and strong wind rent the mountains, and brake in pieces the rocks before the LORD; but the LORD was not in the wind: and after the wind an earthquake; but the LORD was not in the earthquake. 1 KINGS 19:11

168) Raised from the Dead

But Peter put them all forth, and kneeled down, and prayed; and turning him to the body said, Tabitha, arise. And she opened her eyes: and when she saw Peter, she sat up. And he gave her his hand, and lifted her up, and when he had called the saints and widows, presented her alive. ACTS 9:40–41

And as Paul was long preaching, he sunk down with sleep, and fell down from the third loft, and was taken up dead. And Paul went down, and fell on him, and embracing him said, Trouble not yourselves; for his life is in him.
ACTS 20:9–10

169) Taking an Offering

Every man according as he purposeth in his heart, so let him give; not grudgingly, or of necessity: for God loveth a cheerful giver. 2 CORINTHIANS 9:7

Bring ye all the tithes into the storehouse, that there may be meat in mine house, and prove me now herewith, saith the LORD of hosts, if I will not open you the windows of heaven, and pour you out a blessing, that there shall not be room enough to receive it. MALACHI 3:10

170) Quotable Ezra

All such as had separated themselves unto them from the filthiness of the heathen of the land, to seek the LORD God of Israel, did eat, and kept the feast of unleavened bread seven days with

joy. EZRA 6:21–22

But many of the priests and Levites and chief of the fathers, who were ancient men, that had seen the first house, when the foundation of this house was laid before their eyes, wept with a loud voice; and many shouted aloud for joy: So that the people could not discern the noise of the shout of joy from the noise of the weeping of the people.
EZRA 3:12–13

171) Troublemakers

And there was no water for the congregation: and they gathered themselves together against Moses and against Aaron. And the people chode with Moses, and spake, saying, Would God that we had died when our brethren died before the LORD! NUMBERS 20:2–3

And the earth opened her mouth, and swallowed them up together with Korah, when that company died, what time the fire devoured two hundred and fifty men: and they became a sign.
NUMBERS 26:10

172) The Second Coming

And then shall appear the sign of the Son of man in heaven: and then shall all the tribes of the earth mourn, and they shall see the Son of man coming in the clouds of heaven with power and great glory. MATTHEW 24:30

But of that day and that hour knoweth no man, no, not the angels which are in heaven, neither the Son, but the Father. Take ye heed, watch and pray: for ye know not when the time is.
MARK 13:32–33

173) A Common Woman's Name

Is not this the carpenter's son? is not his mother called Mary? and his brethren, James, and Joses, and Simon, and Judas? MATTHEW 13:55

And when the sabbath was past, Mary

Magdalene, and Mary the mother of James, and Salome, had bought sweet spices, that they might come and anoint him. MARK 16:1

174) God Provides

Consider the lilies how they grow: they toil not, they spin not; and yet I say unto you, that Solomon in all his glory was not arrayed like one of these. LUKE 12:27

I have been young, and now am old; yet have I not seen the righteous forsaken, nor his seed begging bread. PSALM 37:25

175) Important Questions

Fear ye not, neither be afraid: have not I told thee from that time, and have declared it? ye are even my witnesses. Is there a God beside me? yea, there is no God; I know not any. ISAIAH 44:8

But when the Pharisees had heard that he had put the Sadducees to silence, they were gathered together. Then one of them, which was a lawyer, asked him a question, tempting him, and saying, Master, which is the great commandment in the law? MATTHEW 22:34–36

176) Martyrs

And they stoned Stephen, calling upon God, and saying, Lord Jesus, receive my spirit. And he kneeled down, and cried with a loud voice, Lord, lay not this sin to their charge. And when he had said this, he fell asleep. ACTS 7:59–60

They were stoned, they were sawn asunder, were tempted, were slain with the sword: they wandered about in sheepskins and goatskins; being destitute, afflicted, tormented; (of whom the world was not worthy). HEBREWS 11:37–38

177) Dreamers

And Pharaoh said unto Joseph, I have dreamed a dream, and there is none

that can interpret it: and I have heard say of thee, that thou canst understand a dream to interpret it. GENESIS 41:15

And he told it to his father, and to his brethren: and his father rebuked him, and said unto him, What is this dream that thou hast dreamed? Shall I and thy mother and thy brethren indeed come to bow down ourselves to thee to the earth? GENESIS 37:10

178) A Word from Amos

For, lo, he that formeth the mountains, and createth the wind, and declareth unto man what is his thought, that maketh the morning darkness, and treadeth upon the high places of the earth, The LORD, The God of hosts, is his name. AMOS 4:13

Therefore the flight shall perish from the swift, and the strong shall not strengthen his force, neither shall the mighty deliver himself: neither shall he stand that handleth the bow; and he that is swift of foot shall not deliver himself: neither shall he that rideth the horse deliver himself. AMOS 2:14–15

179) The Opposite of Proud

Notwithstanding Hezekiah humbled himself for the pride of his heart, both he and the inhabitants of Jerusalem, so that the wrath of the LORD came not upon them in the days of Hezekiah. 2 CHRONICLES 32:26

Thou art snared with the words of thy mouth, thou art taken with the words of thy mouth. Do this now, my son, and deliver thyself, when thou art come into the hand of thy friend; go, humble thyself, and make sure thy friend. PROVERBS 6:2–3

180) Guilty!

Now we know that what things soever the law saith, it saith to them who are under the law: that every mouth may be stopped, and all the world may be-

come guilty before God. ROMANS 3:19

But if ye have respect to persons, ye commit sin, and are convinced of the law as transgressors. For whosoever shall keep the whole law, and yet offend in one point, he is guilty of all. JAMES 2:9–10

181) Forgiven!

For as the heaven is high above the earth, so great is his mercy toward them that fear him. As far as the east is from the west, so far hath he removed our transgressions from us. PSALM 103:11–12

If we say that we have fellowship with him, and walk in darkness, we lie, and do not the truth: But if we walk in the light, as he is in the light, we have fellowship one with another, and the blood of Jesus Christ his Son cleanseth us from all sin. 1 JOHN 1:6–7

182) Gossip and Slander

For I fear, lest, when I come, I shall not find you such as I would, and that I shall be found unto you such as ye would not: lest there be debates, envyings, wraths, strifes, backbitings, whisperings, swellings, tumults. 2 CORINTHIANS 12:20

Lord, who shall abide in thy tabernacle? who shall dwell in thy holy hill? He that walketh uprightly, and worketh righteousness, and speaketh the truth in his heart. He that backbiteth not with his tongue, nor doeth evil to his neighbour. PSALM 15:1–3

183) What the World Needs Most

Owe no man any thing, but to love one another: for he that loveth another hath fulfilled the law. ROMANS 13:8

Seeing ye have purified your souls in obeying the truth through the Spirit unto unfeigned love of the brethren, see that ye love one another with a pure heart fervently: being born again, not of corruptible seed, but of incorruptible, by the word of God. 1 PETER 1:22–23

184) Biblical Skyscrapers

Or those eighteen, upon whom the tower in Siloam fell, and slew them, think ye that they were sinners above all men that dwelt in Jerusalem? I tell you, Nay: but, except ye repent, ye shall all likewise perish. LUKE 13:4–5

Go to, let us make brick, and burn them thoroughly. And they had brick for stone, and slime had they for morter. And they said, Go to, let us build us a city and a tower, whose top may reach unto heaven; and let us make us a name, lest we be scattered abroad. GENESIS 11:3–4

185) Advice from James

Even so faith, if it hath not works, is dead, being alone. Yea, a man may say, Thou hast faith, and I have works: shew me thy faith without thy works, and I will shew thee my faith by my works. JAMES 2:17–18

From whence come wars and fightings among you? come they not hence, even of your lusts that war in your members? Ye lust, and have not: ye kill, and desire to have, and cannot obtain: ye fight and war, yet ye have not, because ye ask not. JAMES 4:1–2

186) More Advice from James

Whereas ye know not what shall be on the morrow. For what is your life? It is even a vapour, that appeareth for a little time, and then vanisheth away. For that ye ought to say, If the Lord will, we shall live, and do this, or that. JAMES 4:14–15

Be patient therefore, brethren, unto the coming of the Lord. Behold, the husbandman waiteth for the precious fruit of the earth, and hath long patience for it, until he receive the early and latter rain. Be ye also patient; stablish your hearts: for the coming of the Lord

draweth nigh. JAMES 5:7–8

187) Doubting Thomas

Then saith he to Thomas, Reach hither thy finger, and behold my hands; and reach hither thy hand, and thrust it into my side: and be not faithless, but believing. JOHN 20:27

Jesus saith unto him, Thomas, because thou hast seen me, thou hast believed: Blessed are they that have not seen, and yet have believed. JOHN 20:29

188) True Motivation

And whatsoever ye do in word or deed, do all in the name of the Lord Jesus, giving thanks to God and the Father by him. COLOSSIANS 3:17

But thou, O man of God, flee these things; and follow after righteousness, godliness, faith, love, patience, meekness. 1 TIMOTHY 6:11

189) A Biblical Queen

And when the queen of Sheba heard of the fame of Solomon concerning the name of the LORD, she came to prove him with hard questions. 1 KINGS 10:1

The queen of the south shall rise up in the judgment with the men of this generation, and condemn them: for she came from the utmost parts of the earth to hear the wisdom of Solomon; and, behold, a greater than Solomon is here. LUKE 11:31

190) Trees

And they heard the voice of the LORD God walking in the garden in the cool of the day: and Adam and his wife hid themselves from the presence of the LORD God amongst the trees of the garden. GENESIS 3:8

Thou shalt not plant thee a grove of any trees near unto the altar of the LORD thy God, which thou shalt make thee. DEUTERONOMY 16:21

191) When Life Doesn't Make Sense

For my thoughts are not your thoughts, neither are your ways my ways, saith the LORD. For as the heavens are higher than the earth, so are my ways higher than your ways, and my thoughts than your thoughts. ISAIAH 55:8–9

Then Job answered the LORD, and said, I know that thou canst do every thing, and that no thought can be withholden from thee. Who is he that hideth counsel without knowledge? therefore have I uttered that I understood not; things too wonderful for me, which I knew not. JOB 42:1–3

192) Rock and Roll

Whoso diggeth a pit shall fall therein: and he that rolleth a stone, it will return upon him. PROVERBS 26:27

And, behold, there was a great earthquake: for the angel of the Lord descended from heaven, and came and rolled back the stone from the door, and sat upon it. MATTHEW 28:2

193) What a Waste. . .

Vanity of vanities, saith the Preacher, vanity of vanities; all is vanity. What profit hath a man of all his labour which he taketh under the sun? ECCLESIASTES 1:2–3

For what is a man profited, if he shall gain the whole world, and lose his own soul? or what shall a man give in exchange for his soul? MATTHEW 16:26

194) Gimme a Sign

And Simeon blessed them, and said unto Mary his mother, Behold, this child is set for the fall and rising again of many in Israel; and for a sign which shall be spoken against. LUKE 2:34

But he answered and said unto them, An evil and adulterous generation seeketh after a sign; and there shall no sign be given to it, but the sign of the prophet Jonas. MATTHEW 12:39

195) Bible Study

Search the scriptures; for in them ye think ye have eternal life: and they are they which testify of me. JOHN 5:39

And the brethren immediately sent away Paul and Silas by night unto Berea: who coming thither went into the synagogue of the Jews. These were more noble than those in Thessalonica, in that they received the word with all readiness of mind, and searched the scriptures daily. ACTS 17:10–11

196) God's Wealth

The silver is mine, and the gold is mine, saith the LORD of hosts. HAGGAI 2:8

For every beast of the forest is mine, and the cattle upon a thousand hills. I know all the fowls of the mountains: and the wild beasts of the field are mine. If I were hungry, I would not tell thee: for the world is mine, and the fulness thereof. PSALM 50:10–12

197) Dirty Birds

And these are they which ye shall have in abomination among the fowls; they shall not be eaten, they are an abomination: the eagle, and the ossifrage, and the ospray. LEVITICUS 11:13

I will give thee unto the ravenous birds of every sort, and to the beasts of the field to be devoured. EZEKIEL 39:4

198) Nice Birds

Are not two sparrows sold for a farthing? and one of them shall not fall on the ground without your Father. MATTHEW 10:29

The flowers appear on the earth; the time of the singing of birds is come, and the voice of the turtle is heard in our land. SONG OF SOLOMON 2:12

199) Important Terms

And he is the propitiation for our sins: and not for ours only, but also for the sins of the whole world. 1 JOHN 2:2

Who was delivered for our offences, and was raised again for our justification. ROMANS 4:25

200) Thoughts on Prayer

My voice shalt thou hear in the morning, O LORD; in the morning will I direct my prayer unto thee, and will look up. PSALM 5:3

The sacrifice of the wicked is an abomination to the LORD: but the prayer of the upright is his delight. PROVERBS 15:8

201) Jesus' Power

All things were created by him, and for him: And he is before all things, and by him all things consist. COLOSSIANS 1:16–17

That at the name of Jesus every knee should bow, of things in heaven, and things in earth, and things under the earth. PHILIPPIANS 2:10

202) Saving the Best for Last

Then Simon Peter answered him, Lord, to whom shall we go? thou hast the words of eternal life. JOHN 6:68

Thou wilt shew me the path of life: in thy presence is fulness of joy; at thy right hand there are pleasures for evermore. PSALM 16:11